THE ULTIMATE MEDICINE

Titles in the **Robert Powell Advaita Library**
from Blue Dove Press:

Sri Nisargadatta Maharaj titles edited by Robert Powell:
The Ultimate Medicine
The Nectar of Immortality
The Experience of Nothingness

Other Robert Powell Advaita Library titles:
Dialogues on Reality
Discovering the Realm Beyond Appearance
Path Without Form
Beyond Religion

Robert Powell Advaita Library titles available Fall 2001:
Return to Meaningfulness (Revised and Expanded)
The Essence of Sri Nisargadatta

Other Titles by Robert Powell:

Zen and Reality
Crisis in Consciousness
The Free Mind
J. Krishnamurti - The Man and His Teaching
The Great Awakening
The Blissful Life
Why Does God Allow Suffering?
Talks with Ramana Maharshi (Editor)
The Essence of Ramana Maharshi (Compiler)

THE ULTIMATE MEDICINE

As Prescribed by
Sri Nisargadatta Maharaj

Edited by Robert Powell, Ph.D.

Foreword by Peter Madill, M.D.

BLUE DOVE PRESS
SAN DIEGO, CALIFORNIA • 2001

The mission of the Blue Dove Foundation is to deepen the spiritual life of all by making available works on the lives, messages, and examples of saints and sages of all religions and traditions as well as other spiritual titles that provide tools for inner growth. These books are distributed in our *Lights of Grace* catalog, our bookstore, and also on our website: www.bluedove.org. For a free catalog contact:

THE BLUE DOVE FOUNDATION
4204 Sorrento Valley Blvd. Suite K
San Diego, CA 92121
Phone: 800-691-1008 or 858-623-3330
E-mail: bdp@bluedove.org
www.bluedove.org

Third printing, 2001

Cover and text design: Brian Moucka
Cover photo courtesy Dingeman Boot
Copy edited by Lawrence Grinnell

ISBN: 1-884997-09-0 (perfect bound)

Printed in Canada

A Dutch edition of *The Ultimate Medicine* has been published under the title *De Ultieme Werkelijkheid*, by Altimira, Heemstede, Holland

Library of Congress Cataloging in Publication data:
Nisargadatta, Maharaj, 1897-1981
    The ultimate medicine / as prescribed by Sri
Nisargadatta Maharaj:
edited by Robert Powell ; foreword by Peter Madill.
     p.   cm.
    Includes bibliographical references.
    ISBN: 1-884997-09-0
    1.Spiritual life--Hinduism. I.Powell, Robert,
1918-.
    BL 1237.36.N578   1994
    294.5'44--dc20   94-34676
                                          CIP

All paths lead to unreality. Paths are creations within the scope of knowledge. Therefore, paths and movements cannot transport you into Reality, because their function is to enmesh you within the dimension of knowledge, while the Reality prevails prior to it.

Sri Nisargadatta Maharaj

ACKNOWLEDGEMENT

First and foremost, I owe a debt of gratitude to my wife Gina who took precious time off from her busy professional career to help me transcribe the tape recordings of these conversations into intelligible English. Her contribution in this matter has indeed been invaluable. I am also grateful for her general encouragement in my undertaking this project.

Secondly, I want to express my thanks to Professors Willard Johnson, of the Department of Religious Studies, San Diego State University, and Lance Nelson, of the Department of Religious Studies, University of San Diego, for help given in the compilation of the Glossary.

Thirdly, I am grateful to Dr. Peter V. Madill, of Sebastopol, California, for making available the original tapes of discourses for this book and for writing its foreword.

And last, but not least, I express my appreciation to Jeff Blom, my publisher, without whose vision and encouragement this work would not have been realized at this time.

The Editor

CONTENTS

FOREWORD

It was a great privilege to visit Sri Nisargadatta Maharaj a little more than a year before his death in September 1981. My journey had not been made on a whim, as prior to that I had been studying his teachings for several years. And, as also had happened to many others, I found myself with an irresistible urge to spend time in his physical presence.

The Maharaj I met was clearly a very old man, in his early eighties. Despite that, he struck me by his energy and vigor, and above all by his relentless passion for sharing his understanding. I also noticed the warm welcome he extended to those with a genuine desire to learn from him, although this did not preclude sharp words or pointed criticisms directed at those who only wanted to show off their book learning or self-assumed importance.

My memories of the events are today as vivid as if they had happened yesterday, and the precept of a truly human yet utterly liberating spirituality remains the guiding beacon in my life. I will forever remain indebted to this remarkable, unpretentious, but clearly fully realized soul for all that he gave and continues to give me.

The talks found in this volume are carefully edited transcripts of the tapes made of conversations I and others had with Maharaj. Lately, there has been some argument as to which of his published works best represents the essence of the teachings, since it had become apparent that in the works following *I Am That* Maharaj, given his age and medical condition, was addressing his visitors much more tersely and with less patience—a teaching style from which some of his followers appear to be drawing erroneous conclusions. To mix metaphors for a moment, I would therefore advise any intending student of Maharaj's teachings to make as his main course a profound study of *I Am That* and enhance this meal with the fine wines of Robert Powell's thoughtfully and devotedly edited later volumes. It has been my experience that many who study this kind of teaching seem to be under the impression that merely listening to an intellectual commentary and a little subsequent reflection on them, to the point of acceptance, automatically grants them realization. Nothing could be further from the truth. Rather I believe that a clear and detailed intellectual grasp of the teaching is essential but still only a first step. Next, students must reflect on the meaning of these teachings, to see how they contradict and undermine the assumptions made about themselves that are acted out in their everyday lives in a search for happiness and fulfillment.

The final and most significant step is the single-minded application and translation of this initial intellectual understanding into the "inner work" and a profound behavioral and attitudinal change; that is, the transformation of our limited, self-defining consciousness into the unbounded and unfettered awareness that is the Self of all. This, I believe, is the essence of spiritual emancipation.

My strong feeling is that Sri Nisargadatta Maharaj will be increasingly recognized as a wholly admirable star in the spiritual firmament of our age. I pray that Robert Powell will see his considerable efforts result in a still wider appreciation of Sri Nisargadatta Maharaj's wisdom, and I add my vote of thanks to him for all his fine work in this area.

Peter V. Madill, M.D.
Sebastopol, California

PREFACE

Most of the discourses presented in these pages were given within the last year before Sri Nisargadatta Maharaj's death and can therefore be considered, like those published in *The Nectar of the Lord's Feet*, as the final teachings in more than one sense of the word. They are characterized by Maharaj's desire, in the waning days of his life, to address only the key issues involved and to do so on the deepest level possible. One cannot help but detect a great sense of urgency and a desire to economize on his dwindling physical energy. This did not allow him to give much time to beginners in dealing with repetitive questions and elementary principles—what Maharaj used to call "kindergarten spirituality."

Some readers of the earlier Nisargadatta books have told me they have noticed several inconsistencies in the material. They must bear in mind, however, that it does not concern a textbook of spirituality; these writings present a record of private conversations with a wide variety of inquirers with greatly different backgrounds, levels of spiritual development and capacities for understanding. Maharaj addressed each of his visitors according to his particular needs and circumstances. Thus, one person might be told to do a lot of meditation, and another, more advanced student, that there is no need for this at all and, in fact, it would be quite useless. He also used words in a very flexible way to suit the occasion. Whereas in the field of science and philosophy, absolute consistency may be regarded as a desirable goal, in the area of spirituality such a requirement would indicate an inappropriate approach to a far deeper and subtler subject, and a sign of remaining ignorance. My advice to readers, therefore, is to accept the material in a holistic manner rather than attempting a microscopic, comparative, and analytical evaluation of textual components. One's openness or receptivity may well hold the key to any spiritual progress.

Robert Powell
La Jolla, California
August 1994

PUBLISHER'S FOREWORD

I was staying in Anandashram in Kanhangad, Kerala, Southern India in 1993. While there one day, a humble kitchen worker, Nithyananda Shenoy, came up to talk with me, as he often did. He handed me a book that he asked me to look at. Initially I had no interest in it but just to be polite I took it from him. The book happened to be the great classic by Sri Nisargadatta Maharaj, *I Am That*.

Upon reading it I realized this was a work of great spiritual power and depth. After that, each time Shenoy visited me, he emphatically said that it was very important for me to publish Maharaj's work in America.

I was very inspired by Maharaj and believed he deserved much more recognition in the West than he was getting. Since it is the mission of Blue Dove Press to promote the lives and messages of sages and saints of all religions, I felt he would certainly be a foremost candidate for our publishing program. I went to Bombay to talk with the Indian publisher, but was informed that the American rights to *I Am That* were already held by Acorn Press.

Several months later, I was back in the U.S. when I was contacted by Robert Powell. He was looking for a suitable publisher for three manuscripts he had edited by Nisargadatta Maharaj. Strangely enough, he contacted

Blue Dove Press, though other publishers were interested. After having a look at these wonderful manuscripts I jumped at the opportunity to make them available in the United States. I am pleased and proud that Robert Powell has chosen us as his publisher for these and other books by him.

In addition to this volume, the Blue Dove Foundation has also published two additional titles of Sri Nisargadatta Maharaj: *The Nectar of Immortality* and *The Experience of Nothingness*.

A friend remarked to me, the lesson is beware of those kitchen workers. You never know when your going to meet another Brother Lawrence!

Jeff Blom
Blue Dove Foundation

THE ULTIMATE MEDICINE

Editor's Notes:

The basic truth of what the great *advaita* masters teach is essentially the same, which is to be expected since there is only one Reality. However, different teachers lay different emphasis on various aspects of this teaching and to this purpose employ slightly different nomenclatures or use these terms in flexible ways as it suits their purposes.

Thus, **I-am-ness** and **beingness** in these conversations are generally used by Maharaj as denoting limited states of understanding which are fundamentally based on a sense of separate identity, resulting from taking oneself to be the body. They are wholly conceptual. Often, Maharaj uses both terms interchangeably. At other times, depending upon the emphasis he wishes to convey, he denotes beingness as a somewhat superior state, which arises upon transcendence of the "I-am-ness" and equates the manifest consciousness. Maharaj also refers to beingness as **consciousness** or **knowingness** and according to him it still is the product of the five elements (rooted in materiality). Thus, he states: "This knowledge 'I am' or the 'beingness' is a cloak of illusion over the Absolute. Therefore, when Brahman is transcended only the *Parabrahman* is, in which there is not even a trace of the knowledge 'I am'." The state[1] of "beingness" is clearly an incomplete, provisional state of understanding, as is also evinced from Maharaj's following words: "The sages and prophets recognized the sense of 'being' initially. Then they meditated and abided in it and finally transcended it, resulting in their ultimate realization."

Whereas "I-am-ness," "beingness" or "knowingness" has a somatic basis, which in turn arises from the physical elements, the Absolute lies beyond all "physicality" and can no longer be described. In the Absolute one has no instrument to make any statements. What I am in the absolute sense, it is not possible to convey in any words. In that ultimate awareness, nobody has any consciousness of being present. The presence itself is not there in the Absolute.

Maharaj teaches that upon transcendence of the individual consciousness into the universal manifest consciousness, the latter rests upon and lies within the Unmanifest or *Parabrahman*, where the latter

---

[1] The term "state" implies a "condition," a modification, of a more basic reality, which concerns an unalterable and ineffable substrate. Therefore, it would be more accurate to express this modification as a superimposition on the "non-state" of the *Parabrahman*, somewhat analagous to the seeing of a snake in the rope.

denotes "that principle which was unaffected by the dissolution of the universes" and is a non-state. He also declares: "Please apprehend this clearly that You, the Absolute—bereft of any body identity—are complete, perfect and the Unborn." In his teaching, you—as the Absolute—never have or had any birth. All forms are a result of the five-elemental play.

This *Parabrahman* lies beyond both duality and non-duality, since it is prior to space and time (we can only properly talk of duality or non-duality within the physical-mental sphere, i.e. within consciousness.) It is the Absolute or the Ultimate Subject, what one *is*, for there is no longer anyone or anything—not even the consciousness—to experience it.

Finally, it must be noted here that other sages as well as classic Vedanta scriptures are commonly using "I-am-ness" and Beingness (spelled with a capital B) interchangeably with the *Parabrahman* or Absolute, and the Absolute is then referred to as Consciousness (with a capital C) and consistently denoted by the term "Self" (Sri Ramana Maharshi) and as the "I-Principle" (Sri Atmananda).

> Even this consciousness is not everything and it is not going to last for all time. Find out how that consciousness has arisen, the source of the consciousness... What is this body? The body is only an accumulation of food and water. Therefore, you are something separate from either the body or the consciousness.
>
> *Sri Nisargadatta Maharaj*

> *Jivatman* is the one who identifies with the body-mind as an individual separate from the world. The *atman* is only beingness, or the consciousness, which is the world. The Ultimate principle which knows this beingness cannot be named at all. It cannot be approached or conditioned by any words. That is the Ultimate state.
>
> *Sri Nisargadatta Maharaj*

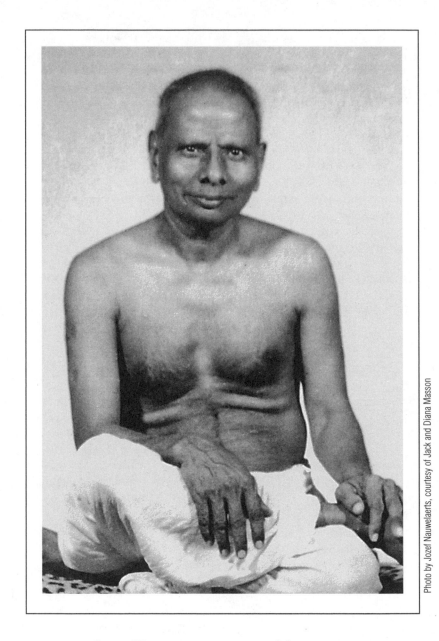

Photo by Jozef Nauwelaerts, courtesy of Jack and Diana Masson

SRI NISARGADATTA MAHARAJ
1897 – 1981

1.

STAY PUT IN BEINGNESS AND ALL DESIRE TO *BE* WILL MELT AWAY

𝕸 **AHARAJ:** That knowledge which experienced itself as Krishna, Buddha or Christ has subsided, it has become one with the Whole.[1] So if you abuse Christ, if you abuse Mohammed, if you abuse anyone, he does not come and ask you: "Why are you abusing me?" because that knowledge, that experience, has mixed with the totality. Similarly, now, you may be a very great person, you might be a dictator of the world, but when you go to sleep you forget what you were—your name, your body, your age, your sex, your nationality, everything. This sense of a separate identity is very limited and not the truth; in fact, it is totally false. So if that is the situation with Christ, what is the case with you?

Or you may be a humble, virtuous person. Whenever you go to sleep, you forget sin, virtue; you forget yourself. What is the basic fact? It is that you forgot yourself as an individual, which gives you deep rest.

When you go to sleep, you might have had sex with a hundred women or a hundred men. At that time you were

---

1 Maharaj views manifestation as the spatio-temporal expression of consciousness. When this consciousness turns in on itself, the avatars or incarnations reflect the highest insight and this Maharaj calls "knowledge." See also Maharaj's remarks on seeing everything as knowledge, on p. 174

enjoying it. But when you sleep, when you take rest, that sensory experience is not there. So then you don't have an identity, no weight at that place. Don't say you are so and so, you are an individual, you are a man or a woman. Just stay put; from there you can move ahead. That is the truth, that is the fact; from there you can go to reality. And then whatever is manifested, will arise and subside. It is like sunrise and sunset, waxing and waning. That desultory manifestation you cannot be; it cannot be the real You.[2]

Whenever there is a sense of individuality, personality, or a separateness, you have so many wants. You want to see a movie, you want to hear music, you want to play, you want to have sex, you want to eat fancy foods, you want to consume intoxicant, but when that sense of separateness is not there, when you are one with the totality, these things are not desired. And spirituality or what you call "religion" is mainly to understand this: that you don't require anything, you are a part of the totality, or reality. When you grasp that, you don't have any of these needs. But so long as you are separate from things, you need everything.

To exist as a separate individual constitutes the entire problem. And all these things, the various sense caterings, all reading, search for knowledge, for pleasure, everything is related to that. Once all that subsides, there is no more problem. Then the bliss you experience is true bliss. The foregoing, however, is not a ban on activities. Do whatever you want, but never forget the reality, never forget what you really are. You are not the body, you are not the food, you are not this vital air *(prana)*. Whatever has appeared is a state, and as such it has to go.

Most of you are not going to understand what is being said here, because you are taking yourself to be the body. Whatever knowledge I am conveying is not directed to the body—with you as bodily entities, as different persons.

---

2 What one is must have a permanent identity; so it certainly is not this.

So long as you are firmly convinced that you are the body, whatever I am telling you is not going to be of any use to you. Because whatever knowledge we take, we take it as body-mind, since it adds to our existing store of information. We then feel we have become more knowledgeable. For example, tomorrow some astrologer or palmist may want to come and tell me: I would like to tell your future. How can he tell my future, when I am not there at all? You would be happy when told, OK, you will be President of the United States. But with me that is not the case.

In various books, they have written about God. Has anyone said what God looks like, what he is really like? Has he got a shape, certain qualities? A God with attributes is still time-bound. Once time comes to an end, even his knowledge of being God vanishes. Just like a beggar dressed as a king, he may feel as a king so long as he wears king's clothes. Once he throws away the clothes, he knows he is a beggar.

When we talk about God, we are referring to attributes—loving, omnipresent, omniscient, and so on...yet all that is still time-bound. Once that experience goes, what is there left? Well, anything that has got attributes cannot be lasting. This is very clear to me. So what then can I ask for myself?

Whatever behavior exists in this world, it is because of attributes, tendencies. For example, a person goes through four marriages and divorces in a month. Now that behavior stems from tendencies, qualities. But that which witnesses this behavior is beyond attributes. When that witness itself, which is "I am," subsides, what remains? With the witness gone, all other things have disappeared, too. By the same token, upon the arising of the "I am," the whole of manifestation takes place; these two are not separate, they are one. "I am" is the witness; the entire manifest world is there because of this.

That which is doing all this are the tendencies or attributes, or *maya*. Just like the sun and its rays: if the sun is not there, the rays are absent. Similarly, if the witness is not there, the manifestation or *maya* is not present. When "I am" arises, everything appears; when "I am" subsides, everything subsides. Now this is what I am trying to tell you, but you want something else. You want something about your future, something which is part of manifestation, but I am trying to hit at it.

You have been seeing me right from 5:30 in the morning—working, talking and doing all that. But nowhere am I aware of myself as a *jnani*, as something different. On the other hand, I have not forgotten the child of many years ago. Now eighty-two years back, I had the childish knowledge, the incomplete knowledge, which was born from the ignorance that I was born. Until the age of three, I did not know anything. After that age, I was struck by my mother with what is a word, you know, concepts, and out of those concepts everything else came. Now this *maya* is that which started eighty-two years ago; it is singing. *Maya* comes up, subsides again; it goes in cycles, waxing and waning. Now after some time, this childish knowledge, incomplete knowledge, whose base is ignorance...that experience which started eighty-two years ago—let us not call it an identity—will also pass away, wither away.

This "I am" is an announcement; it is not the real. It has come out of something else. What the real is, I am not telling you, because words negate that. Whatever I am telling you, is not the truth, because it has come out of that "I am." The fact is, I cannot describe reality to you, I cannot explain it, because it is beyond expression. So from that, everything flows; but every time I say something, I am aware that it is to be negated, "not this, not this" *(neti-neti)*...that is my experience. And further, I have not seen God, have not seen anything else. But about my own experience, I am very sure, and that is what I am telling you about; I am not quoting anyone.

Because that food-body is there, and that slice of bread, the "I-am-ness" appears. Since this is dependent on the body, it is ignorance; therefore, this "I-am-ness" knowledge cannot remain permanently, it is a function of this food-body. So long as the food-body is present, this "I-am-ness" will remain. Thereafter, it will go.

As was said before, the same child knowledge, that "I-am-ness," still persists. The "I-am-ness" view appeared in the child body, as it is here today. But because of *maya*, continuous changes take place; the situation has changed but "I-am-ness" still continues. For how long? For so long as the food-body is viable. When the food-body is dropped by the vital breath, the "I-am-ness" will set. So "I-am-ness" is not permanent either; the consciousness is not permanent.

Our prime minister has some firm ideas about himself and whatever concepts he entertains. He does not want to change them—ideas of God, etc. We human beings have so many pet notions, preconceived ideas. Whenever we listen to somebody whose idea tallies with ours, we agree. Otherwise, we reject. Similarly, those *jnanis* who state they are established in the Absolute are actually in beingness. They are known as sages. They like certain ideas, certain concepts, and they want to propagate those. But they propagate only "idea," and an idea is not the truth. Truth is the state beyond concepts.

You take the seed of the banyan tree. It is very small, smaller than the mustard seed. The seed is very subtle, but all the gross matter is already inside it. Do you see the paradox? Similarly, your essential being is the subtlest, yet it contains the whole universe. Another point is, what do you mean by seed? *Bija* means "second creation" and thus signifies that the past is being repeated. It was a tree; the tree got concentrated in the seed; and the seed re-creates the past history it contains.

VISITOR: The "I am" is in the seed. At this point, when one is aware of the "I am," the seed, to become the Absolute...

M: You are itself the seed, you are "I-am-ness." You don't grossify it even by words. The inner core, the self, what is inside? All this[3] is inside that seed!

V: Maharaj also said that the inner core is light.

M: No, light here is meant only symbolically. It is not light like this...Self-luminous.

Everything is truth, the Absolute. This *Brahman* is created out of your beingness. All this *Brahman* is illusion, born out of ignorance, for your beingness, from the Absolute standpoint, is ignorance only. Again, out of ignorance, this beingness develops everything, the entire manifestation. On the Absolute, beingness appears and out of that comes illusion, and the illusion occupies the truth.

V: So what is our way of reversing this process?

M: Recede, recede. The lion wherever he goes, looks back. Like that, look back, go to the source, the seed.

When you pursue the spiritual path, the path of self-knowing, all your desires, all your attachments, will just drop away, provided you investigate and hold on to that with which you are trying to understand the self. Then what happens? Your "I-am-ness" is the state "to be." You are "to be" and attached to that state. You love to be. Now, as I said, in this inquiry your desires drop off. And what is the primary desire? To *be*. When you stay put in that beingness for some time, that desire also will drop off. This is very important. When this is dropped off, you are in the Absolute—a most essential state.

V: That is the exact feeling that came over us today. There is a certain sadness in realizing that and yet a

---

3 presumably the entire manifestation.

greater understanding of the Absolute.

M: Sadness, because that "I-am-ness" was sad. [*laughter*]

V: You know that there is Being, and you are going towards non-Being. And there are all the things of Being and you know that they are really nothing. But it was fun; it was a great illusion while it lasted.

M: Your true state, stay put in that. It is ever there, in its pure state, undisturbed. Only that consciousness, "I-am-ness," is consciously receding from the Absolute. That "you"...you are present only; there is not the slightest movement from you. It is winding up the show.

V: Would you say that a little more clearly?

M: Yes. When you are in consciousness, you understand the nature of consciousness and you recede. Your progress continues. This consciousness is slowly extinguishing itself; knowingly it is disappearing. But nothing affects You, because that is the Absolute. Just like when the flame is gone, the smoke is gone, the sky remains.

V: Beautifully said!

M: That is the *Brahman* of death, the moment of death. Watching occurs, the vital breath is leaving the body, "I-am-ness" is receding, vanishing. That is the greatest moment, the moment of immortality.

The body, the flame, that "I-am-ness," is there; its movements are there, and I observe. And it is extinguished. The vital breath deserts the body, that flame is not there. You observe that. That observation occurs to you. The ignorant one at the moment of death is in great fright; he is struggling. But not the *jnani*; for him it is the happiest moment, the most blissful one.

But the fact is that you are going all over the place...to saints and ashrams and all that, collecting knowledge in your capacity of being an "individual." Don't do that. Go beyond. This amassing of knowledge is not going to help you, because it is in a dream. This dream will repeat itself, as a human body, as so many other bodies, as an animal or as a god, anything. That is not the point. Try to understand what is being said here. That only is the solution and will lead you somewhere.

What is the relationship between me and you? I don't care whether or not you come here and listen. If you find it, you take it; if you don't want it, go away. The space in this room is neither against nor for, nor in love with, the space in that other room. It is one. Similarly, I am not bothered.

The knowledge I am giving out is like a stream, like a flowing river. If you want to utilize it, take the water, drink it, assimilate it. Let it flow by itself. I am not charging you anything. You are spending a lot of money every day. Come on, you keep the money and take my water.

Similarly, while talking about it I take you to the source of the spring. There, water is coming out in a trickle now. This trickle subsequently becomes a river, an estuary, and finally the sea. I take you to the source again and again.

Once you arrive at the source, you come to know that actually there is no water. The water is purely the taste, the news that "I am."

This body-mind is created out of mischief. So whenever I say, don't ask from the body-mind consciousness and you comply with that, it means you are out of mischief; you will not ask any more mischievous questions.

After listening to these words and understanding their meaning, stay convinced that you are That, you are the totality. Then, out of that, tremendous blessings will come your way.

You become a *mahayu(k)*;[4] that is, you merge into yourself, union with yourself. There is only one principle; the principle is that "you are." Because you are, everything is. Hold it firmly to yourself.

What is your aim? Do you really want what I am talking about? You have heard what has been said. Now live accordingly, and remain with it.

You are indulging in worldly activity continually. Now before you go to sleep, forget about all that and start reflecting on reality. Because we can all break away from society. And the next thing is: don't run from door to door. I am of the opinion that most of you are doing that, just amassing knowledge; there is no point in that. Take one sentence of what has been said here, and stay with it. That is enough; that will lead you to your source.

My word, as knowledge, if planted in you, will remove all other words, all concepts. So for this purpose, I will tell you a story. One person takes another person to an hotel, makes him eat something. Afterwards he tells him, in six months you are going to die, because I have put some poison in the food. So that fellow gets frightened. He leaves him and meets another friend of his and tells him what has just happened. This man says, don't worry. You see this glass; it is filled with urine. Come on, you drink this. If you do, you will survive, there will be no death for you. So that man drinks it. What happens? He didn't die. So with the first concept, "I am duly poisoned," he is full of fright and convinced that he is going to die after six months. Later this second man gives him another concept, that he is *not* going to die, and he survives, he goes beyond death.

One of the attributes of life, of the vital air, is getting concepts, ideas, creation, over and over again. Who understands this? A person who has searched for himself. Only when you do that, you become aware of all this.

The source of all happiness is your beingness. Establish yourself there, be there. But if you get yourself involved in

---

4 A play on words (since *maha* means great, "a great 'you'").

the flow, then you will come to misery. You understand what is the flow? All that *maya*, the activities. You try to derive pleasure from the activities; this is a product of the illness. Whatever I have told you, reminisce on it, chew it, be still. Because it will lead you to stillness that way.

It will be clear to you that just as with the five fingers of the hand, this body of yours is made of the five elements. Because of the five elements,[4] the body is there. Your being-ness, the consciousness, is the essence of what is to appear as the result of the vital breath which is circulating in the body. And when that consciousness disappears, or the vital breath deserts the body, everything disappears. This should be very clear to you. Just as this spark comes about because of this chemical ingredient [*referring to his cigarette lighter*], everything is present only because this food is there. So you understand that your "I-am-ness" or consciousness is there because of this food body, and because the vital breath is there. And you will be able to watch all these elements: your body, the vital force, and your beingness. When you are in a position to watch all that, you get established in reality.

One can get rid of habits only with considerable difficul-ty. Once the habits are formed, it takes quite some time to get out of them. Similarly, although you have got this knowledge now, what it gives you, you don't know yet. Because you have been associated with the body-mind for such a long period, to get rid of that will take some time. But for you to become established in the knowledge, reflecting and meditating on it is very essential. For that it is necessary to quit one habit you are normally given to and substitute another habit. Now what is this substitute habit? It is to think constantly that you are not the body.

For example, if you engage yourself in a quarrel with

---

4 In Hindu philosophy, the "five elements" — earth, water, fire, air and ether (or space) — are considered to be the fundamental building blocks of the entire physical universe.

somebody, observe and understand clearly that there is a quarrel started by your mind, but you are only its witness. If you don't participate, whether there is a quarrel or not is no longer a concern. All the worldly activities happen through the mind. If you think "I am the body-mind," then you are doomed.

When you are absolutely one with *Brahman*, you don't resort to mind. So there is no sound or you cannot talk. You stay put or keep quiet. To talk, you have to take advantage of this instrument, the mind. So you need to get a little detached from *Brahman*; then only the talk can come out.

January 1, 1979

2.

WHATEVER HAS SPRUNG FROM THE FIVE ELEMENTS IS SHEER IGNORANCE

MAHARAJ: The knowledge "I am" is the same in all sentient creatures, whether it be an insect, a worm or a human being, or even an avatar, the highest kind of being. I do not consider this basic consciousness in one form as being different in any way from the consciousness in another form. But in order to manifest itself, consciousness needs a base, a particular construct in which it can appear. That base can be anything, it may be any form, but the manifestation can last only so long as that particular form endures. And until that consciousness appears, there cannot be knowledge of any kind. In sum, knowledge depends on consciousness, and consciousness needs a physical matrix or form.

One must also consider the importance of the word. The thought arises from the vital breath and expresses itself in the word. Without words, there could not be any communication in the world; in fact, there could not have been any activity, any "busy-ness" (or business, for that matter), at all. The world goes on because of the word and the name. People could not have been identified without name. So the word and the name have great importance.

The principle of naming every possible "thing" has been carried forward to the extent that even God had to be given a name. And that name, when repeated, has a certain significance. At an early stage of one's spiritual development, there is no method, no *sadhana*, more important or effective than repeating the name of God.

Now there exists no particular reason for the coming about of this consciousness. So there is no explanation for how this seed, this consciousness or knowledge "I am," has arisen. But once it is in existence, it cannot stand still—that is, consciousness is tantamount to "movement." And all movement takes place through the *gunas*,[1] which are inherent in the knowledge "I am." This consciousness keeps on "humming"—[*Maharaj uses the Marathi word* gun-gun]—and expresses itself through the three *gunas*. These *gunas* act according to the form which has come about, and that form has resulted from a particular food. Behavior and action result from the combinations and permutations of the three *gunas*.

When people first come here, I always tell them that they come with the purpose of showing off their knowledge or trying to draw me into an argument. So I am aware of that, but I am even more strongly aware of the fact that such people have not got the slightest idea what they are talking about. I call it pure ignorance. It is for this reason that I say, don't ask any questions, don't even start discussing, until you have listened to the talk for a while and absorbed at least some of its contents. Then you can begin asking questions.

How do I know that you are completely ignorant? From my own experience. Any infant will take at least a year, a year and a quarter, or a year and a half, before he can even utter a word. That word may not have any meaning, but to do so, what has happened? Again I am using the word *gun-gun*, that which is going on internally wanting to come out—

---

1 The three *gunas* — *sattva* (purity, clarity, harmony), *rajas* (passion, energy, activity) and *tamas* (inertia, resistance, darkness) — are the basic attributes or qualities that underlie and operate the world process, according to Hindu teachings.

thoughts, odd words, whatever it may be. And it does come out. Now, where did all that originate? Where is the presenter of the speech? Speech is only for animals, which includes humans. Now that is still part of the knowledge "I am," which is within them. This *gun-gun* is within the knowledge "I am," which includes the physical form. The *gun-gun* entity and the knowledge "I am" and the physical form—that whole bundle—has been created out of the five elements. So up to this point, the whole thing can be said to be entirely mechanistic and therefore pure ignorance.

Now there are some people who say: I was so and so in a previous existence. How do they know? They could only have sprung from the five elements. And before the five elements were created, the previous knowledge could not have been there. Therefore, it is utter nonsense, rubbish.

There are many *Hatha*-yogis who have great powers. Of those, I am the greatest. But I distinguish between *Hatha*-yoga and *Hatha*. *Hatha* means "insistence" or "persistence." You see, I *persist*. And what is this persistence about? I did not know that I was going to be born. How did I get this birth? That is the point on which I persist in finding the answer. I *must* know this. When I was told "*sattva*," then what is *sattva*? *Sattva* is the essence of the five elements. In that essence, in that juice, lies the knowledge "I am." But all that is still of the five elements. Then how did this come about? My guru told me the whole story. Thus, I came to know that it is ignorance, and I know from experience that everybody is starting from there. Thus, whatever has come about is sheer ignorance. And we are nothing more, that is what my guru told me.

My guru further pointed out to me the fact that the only thing you have and which you can utilize to unravel the mystery of life, is this knowledge "I am." Without that, there is absolutely nothing. So I got hold of it, as my guru advised me, and then I wanted to find out how the spiritual aspect of "me" came about without my knowledge. That again is the result of the five elements. Therefore, I repeat, I know from personal experience that if anybody thinks he has or is something special, it is sheer ignorance.

Even if this body were to last for a thousand years, any experience with it that has come about during that period is necessarily based on this "I-am-ness," which is based on time, which is a product of the five elements for which I have no use at all. On my pure Absoluteness, which has no place, and no shape or form, this knowledge "I am" came, which also has no shape or form. Therefore, it appears; and it is only an illusion.

Intelligent people, extremely intelligent people, come here and ask me questions. And I answer them. So what happens? They don't accept my replies. Why? Because they ask me from the point of view of identification with the body-mind. And I answer them from a point of view which is without such identification. So how can they understand me? How can the answers possibly tally with the questions?

Who are asking the questions? It is the persons who see themselves as existing in time, with the birth of the physical body as their base point; therefore, they ask questions from that point of view. But that view is false; it is a figment of their imagination—purely a bundle of memories, habits and imagination. They consider that as the truth; yet it is sheer ignorance, having no basis in reality at all. The day to which you are attaching so much importance met you when the body was born, and from that day onward you have been considering yourself as that body.

What was there before the body came into being, only that may remain after the disappearance of the body and the elements. And before that body is gone, on that final day, even the memory of existence during the prior period will disappear. So whatever happens between appearance and disappearance of the body is only a bundle of memories; whatever you have accumulated is merely entertainment. All that is in memory and everything will disappear.

Now if you had really accepted this through proper understanding, you would not care whether this body remains or goes.

When the highest principle, this beingness in the body disappears, how can you talk? When that primary principle has gone, is there any value left? First the beingness is to disappear. Then also, the body will disappear. But the beingness will never know that the body is disappearing, because the beingness itself will already have left.

When a child is born, after a year or two, he is able to talk. From where has this capacity developed? From the food essence of the body only, is it not? Internally, he developed this power of speech.

The Maharishi[2] has over eight thousand disciples, but does he speak of this knowledge? They depend on this beingness as the truth; they take it as the reality. And all deference is being directed toward that beingness; all spiritual activities are based on the feeling that this beingness is the truth. But is it not also the product of the food essence? And, therefore, does it eventually not become decrepit with the food essence?

Don't you understand your knowingness naturally, effortlessly? Once you understand spontaneously, you will realize that it is also a temporary phase: this beingness is going to disappear. And in understanding this, you will come to the conclusion that it is unreal. And the one who understands its unreality is the eternal.

Now, continuing to explore in this vein, can you hold on to some identity that is exclusively yours, that will not disappear? Without the help of some food essence, can anybody talk? And can anybody incarnate himself without the help of a body?

[*Maharaj has just received an invitation to go by car to a village to talk to the people there*] Will anybody be able to

---

2 Maharishi Mahesh Yogi.

understand this kind of talk, what I'm driving at? The problem is, after such a talk, might the people not obtain my address and come to get me? No, the locals may not; they are not such type of people. But the foreigners may try to attack me, because I am criticizing Christ. I have indicated knowing the true position of Christ, because he talks about the same thing.

What was done to Christ might happen to me also, because Christ started telling the facts—the truth. And people got enraged and crucified him—they dared to shed his blood.

Since my talk will be beyond the scope of their understanding, some of the audience may become very upset and disturbed. They will say, it's no use, we must finish him off. It is because of the command of my guru that I am doing this, participating in all these talks. When I go to that village, I will have to discourse about God and purity; I must take the devotional approach. But if I gave the kind of talk that I am giving here, they would not be able to understand it. I should talk on their level of understanding—God, purity, and devotion.

28 March 1980

3.

THE ULTIMATE
MEDICINE

*M*AHARAJ: ...the five *pranas*, *panchapranas*, become purified; concomitantly the sense organs become purified, and the mind also becomes pure. And when the mind is pure, the language of the sages becomes intelligible. Without such purification, it is not possible to understand the sages. And, ultimately, that purification leads to Self-knowledge, to the Self.

VISITOR: Does this purification arise as a consequence of applying oneself to meditation on the sense of "I am"? And is that one's central responsibility?

M: I am referring to what we call the *sattva*, signifying the essence of the food that you consume. This body is nothing but food for the consciousness. Now the quality of this *sattva* is the beingness or the knowledge that we *are*—the "I"-consciousness. And, ultimately, you should know this *sattva*, what it is; but for the moment I will tell you this is the essence of all the food.

Your question was whether through meditation this purification takes place. Yes. And how this happens is that by meditation the *sattva* quality gets predominant, the mind gets purified and then the knowledge of the Self is made possible. Just as the quality of sugar is sweetness, so the quality of this *sattva*, the essence of food, is this knowledge, this "I"-consciousness or, as we also call it, beingness. Just as the sweetness of...

V: How can that be the quality of food? I am just not clear on what you are trying to say. Food can be either very *tamasic* or very *rajasic*; it depends on the food chosen. Are you talking about food in terms of whatever thoughts, instruction, we ingest, or just simply the gross elements we take in?

M: Ultimately the food has taken this form, which is the body. Now in this body, which is nothing but food, an entity called *sattva* is present. There is some connection between this *sattva* and the food. It is not simply that the food is this *sattva*; the latter is some subtle product, some essence of the food. Is that clear?

V: It's becoming clearer.

M: Then there is also something called the *moolasattva*, the origin of *sattva*, original essence. Its quality is that you come to know that you are. So in your body that primordial *sattva*, or *moolasattva*, is present because of which you have the knowledge that you exist.

Another thing concerns so-called "sickness." If anything goes wrong with the *sattva* or the material of the body, there is some disorder which is termed "sickness." How do the doctors rectify that? By giving you medicine; the medicine is also a kind of *sattva*. So that medicine rectifies this disorder and then the sickness is cured.

V: Sometimes.

M: Actually, this beingness or knowingness itself is the misery. Prior to the appearance of the beingness you did not have any problems; they started only after its appearance. To repeat: With the form, the beingness appeared—the knowledge that you exist—and along with that, came all the problems. So this knowingness or beingness is nothing but misery. Any comment on this? Do you agree?

V: I agree with that, yes. Sometimes I feel that illness arises as a lawful consequence of what people do; at other times it just seems to be something built into the body that we do not understand and it just arises; it has a force all of its own. And either it will be dissipated when something counters…

M: Again, this beingness, the knowledge "I am," which I call *upadro*, is the source of trouble. As I said in the morning, as the result of happiness this source of misery has also begun. In this *upadro*, in this primary essence, lies the knowledge "I am"—you know that you are.

V: I have no argument with this.

M: You see, the quintessence of this body essence is ultimately the knowledge "I am." That is sustained by this food-essence body. Do you follow?

V: I follow it…

M: Now, this quintessence that is the knowledge "I am," in the period of a day, there will be moments when miseries are experienced by it. Because it is in its very nature to experience those. Thus, with the appearance or happening of this "I-am-ness," miseries are bound to follow, a natural corollary.

V: They usually outweigh the pleasures.

M: This beingness has two aspects: deep sleep and the waking state. "I-am-ness" means that the waking state is there or the deep sleep state is there. So...

V: How do you mean "I-am-ness" signifies the deep sleep or waking state? I don't understand that.

M: You know in the waking state that you are.

V: In the waking state, yes, I know that I am.

M: When you go to sleep, you do not know that you are. Isn't that so?

V: That's true.

M: So that means these two aspects of "I-am-ness" are always there. In deep sleep, "I-am-ness" is forgotten. And because it is forgotten, you are completely relaxed and at peace with yourself. During the waking state, to know that you are is itself a misery; but since you are preoccupied with so many other things, you are able to sustain that waking state.

This quality of beingness, the knowledge "I am," cannot tolerate itself. It cannot stand itself, alone, just knowing itself. Therefore, that *rajoguna* is there...it takes the beingness for a ride in various activities, so that it does not dwell only in itself; it is very difficult to sustain that state. And *tamoguna* is the basest quality. What it is doing is that it provides one with the facility to claim authorship for all the activities—the feeling "I am the doer." *Rajoguna* takes one into all the activities, and *tamoguna* claims authorship or doership for those activities. But understand fully that whatever is happening takes place because of these three qualities, *sattvaguna*, *rajoguna*, and *tamoguna*. They are not *your* doings, you are completely apart from that. I stress that time and again. This is the play happening in these three *gunas*. Again understand, you are experiencing this *sattvaguna*, the knowledge "I am." This "I-am-ness" is experienced by you, the Absolute, but you are not "I-am-ness." What have you to say on this?

V: What could I say? I don't have any comment.

M: What I am expounding here is not normally expounded anywhere.

V: I know, that is why I am here.

M: Having understood, realized and transcended all these three *gunas*, I know full well their play; that is why I talk like this. I have understood, I have realized, I have transcended them. A number of sages, having done all the expounding, will only take you into *sadhana*, the disciplines that are to be followed. But this is a subject...prior to discipline, subtler than any discipline, a most subtle one.

V: And yet at the same time the activity that he enjoins us to undertake purifies the play of those *gunas* in the sense that they don't keep drawing our attention back into the world. Because, unless there is some responsibility on our part, which Maharaj insists upon as much as anyone else, the play of the three *gunas* will be just random and you will be like a ball kicked around by a bunch of dolphins.

M: By following what was said it will be realized that whatever is happening is happening only in the realm of these *gunas*. And in this process it is realized one is not part of their play at all. Becoming more and more detached from all worldly activities, one transcends the *gunas* and knows one does not dwell in their realm.

When you are involved with the *gunas*, you want to have

so many things from the world; but when you thoroughly understand that you are not these *gunas*, then you want or expect nothing.

V: Is *sadhana* necessary?

M: *Sadhana*, the discipline, is only this: The knowledge which is dwelling in this body, the quintessence of these three *gunas*—the knowledge "I am," "I am that"—this is the initial step. You must be one with it, you must abide in that only. You have to think "I am not the body but I am that formless, nameless knowledge indwelling in this body; that (is) 'I am'."

When you abide sufficiently long in this state, whatever doubts you may have, that knowledge "I am" itself will sprout out with life and meaning for you, intended for you only, and everything will become clear. No external knowledge will be necessary.

V: Is any technique required for the *sadhana*?

M: Only conviction! If you are thinking of any initiation...Only the words of the guru that you are not the body! That is the initiation. Stay put there, in that state.

It is spontaneous, natural, that *shraddha* (faith). What is that faith? "I am," without the words, whatever you are, that itself is the faith. Now you have to elevate yourself to the state of *Brahman*, that "I am" itself is *Brahman*; this is the condition you have to develop.

V: For that, is it necessary to sit in seclusion for a certain period of time?

M: Until you abide in that firm conviction, probably you will have to go into seclusion. But once you abide and stay put firmly there, you know you are that only; then even if you are in a crowd you will not have a fall from that.

V: At the moment when you are realized, you are That; other times, you are only contemplating that you are That, you are trying to believe that you are That. But the moment the conviction comes, is that the realization?

M: Yes, that is the moment to know.

V: So when you are realized, what are the signs of realization?

M: No symbols are available, because only you shall prevail at that moment.

V: But will one see anything specific?

M: You know, surprisingly, there may be so many things you see. You might see lights...All this illumination is due to what? To *atma-jyoti*, the light of the Self, Self-illumination.

V: I have read in several books that simultaneously with the realization, there is an awakening of the *kundalini*. Is this a fact?

M: What you are saying about *kundalini* happens to him. I am not dealing with that.

V: Happens to whom?

M: To the one who is expounding that idea. I don't deal with those concepts. That is Muktananda's sphere.

V: And several other people say the same.

M: My approach is different. I don't expound that.

V: Is the result not the same? Whoever attained realization, we are merely told about it. But there is no actual proof. We are told by the realized yogis, that whenever they got realization, supernatural powers were acquired. Strange lights appeared to them; they went into a different sphere. Something terrific happens to them at the time of realization.

M: You might also have visions of various gods. Anything might happen, but that does not mean that you should dwell on those concepts.

V: Yes, but can those things happen?

M: Yes, but in the process of trying to experience and observe all these things, it is easy to forget the way toward Self-realization. Those people are studying, as it were, on the TV screen; that means they still want to be in an experiential state. They do not transcend that.

V: What Maharaj is expounding, speaking the language of the Gita, is it *jnana-marg*?

M: No, not the *jnana* "path." Abidance in knowledge is different. *Jnana marg* means you are walking a path. Your destination is the knowledge "I am"—abidance in that knowledge.

V: That is, according to the Gita, *jnana*.

M: *Marg* means you are always trying to walk. I do not want to do any walking.

When you talk about "path," you think the destination is far off and you have to walk there. The point is that you are right at the destination, so where is the necessity of any path?

V: Is it easily attainable?

M: Spontaneously, it is the natural state, the destination. Unfortunately, you are connected with various types of concepts, and you are bogged down in the quagmire of those concepts.

As it is, "you are" is most spontaneous and natural.

V: Again, I will put it in another way. In the Gita...

M: I do not want you to seek support in anything external. There are only two entities, you and me. Don't introduce a third person or a third support. The dialogue is strictly between us.

V: What difference is there between you, Maharaj, and Lord Krishna?

M: I don't know what you mean by "difference," for that term does not occur in my vocabulary.

V: So if I quote Lord Krishna of the Gita, for my own satisfaction, is it...if *you* don't enlighten me, who else will?

M: The knowledge "you are" is Lord Krishna.

V: OK. So my knowledge...

M: That is Krishna.

V: My knowledge is that devotion is the easiest way, and either Rama, Krishna or anybody, even Guru, you concentrate on that, don't even think that I am, who I am, this and that, it is better to be an ant than sugar, and with devotion you take his name, the Lord's name. Or the Guru's name. And you get the realization. You even get the *jnana*. By only *bhakti*, blind *bhakti*. Without even thinking who you are, what you are, that knowledge itself, "I am That," will dawn. With conviction, realization will occur.

M: If you have gone through all that, why did you come here? Having done all these things—the devotional path—the knowledge must have dawned in you. Again, one must ask, why did you come?

V: No, the knowledge has not dawned. I feel incomplete. I was not crowing about devotion. I was wanting. So...

M: There is no question of knowledge dawning in you, *because you are that knowledge.* It is already there. That is the only condition.

V: By blind devotion?

M: Why do you want blind devotion, when you are already That?

V: Because it is easiest for ninety-nine percent of the people. I can believe in you more easily than I can believe that I am God. I can believe that you are God, you are more godly. You *are* God. You are *shaktiman.* I can't believe that *I* am *shaktiman.*

M: You will never be alerted to that higher state if you do not believe that you are the God. That is *advaita* devotion. There is no difference between a god and yourself. You are God only. Only I prevail.

V: Yes, I know. But they say even *dvaita* and *advaita*...both will lead you to the Ultimate.

M: A lot of people may say a lot of things. But what I am telling you is this: See that you are and know that you are. Just be that.

V: Is *dvaita* incorrect? Can it lead to the same...?

M: There is no question of duality because nothing exists except me. Only I exist. I deal only with that Highest, whatever it is. In the lower, everything is true, on that level. But I don't deal with that stuff at all. I don't expound the initial stages...That time is over for myself. If anybody places full reliance on my words, that you are the *Brahman*, you are everything, that itself will transform you.

V: Whatever I am is the result of my *prarabdha?*[1]

M: What is that *prarabdha*, that destiny, you are talking about? I know of no *prarabdha*, no destiny. In the initial stages, in the kindergarten thinking of spirituality, I used to say that. To one who is receiving primary initiation into spirituality, for him these lessons are good enough. But not for my *sadhana*. For an advanced course in spirituality, I will not explain this. These concepts are rejected. If you don't like my teachings, whatever I say, you may blame me and are free to leave here.

V: Can a man shape his destiny?

M: I have said already: I don't believe in destiny. If you have been on the path of devotion, where is the necessity of destiny at all? With devotion, individuality has transformed itself into *Brahman*, the manifested. So how is the destiny needed for that? That *Brahman* state, the manifest *Brahman*, is not subject to any destiny. Is there any question of something good or bad happening to that *Brahman* state? He who is not one with the *Brahman* and still thinks he is an individual, will always be thinking that something good or bad is going to happen to him, as an entity conditioned by body-mind.

What have you got to say? Your comments, Sir.

V: One of the things that I feel very strongly is happening in the

---

1 *prarabda:*.karma playing out in one's present life; destiny.

West, through the Eastern teachings from such representatives as Maharaj and Ramana Maharshi, is that people are so aggressive in attaining things, and when they get bored with attaining material benefits and sexual satisfactions and all the transitory pleasures of drugs, they turn to the spiritual life; but their view of spirituality is still conditioned by the same motive for attainment.

M: You have to understand in the West people go towards spirituality because they are getting bored with this objective worldly life. So one must understand what is the cause of the misery. That source you must find out. Is it not necessary?

V: I believe it absolutely is. That is why Maharaj's teaching is so important, because it stands quite apart from the usual teachings...

SECOND VISITOR: I think that what my newfound friend here is still trying to understand is the same basic confusion that we are having much more recently in the West in that people associate realization with attainments relative to this whole *chakra* system, and it is not that at all. You know when Ramana Maharshi was asked about this, he would say the only centre that interested him was the heart.

M: Anybody coming here will be liquidated: he is not going to get anything.

When you reach that state, the highest state, then only will you be realized, whether you are going to attain or discard. I assure you that you will attain nothing and you will realize that no attainment is required. Abide in the words I have spoken earlier. First do your homework, then ask questions.

I would like to know from you, what medicine is there which will help you to know that you are and put to use that knowledge "you are."

V: Maharaj's instruction, that is the only medicine I know.

M: Continue to come here if you want to investigate what you are. Track down what that "you are" is. Investigate that medicine "you are." And don't expose all and sundry to what I have told you. Keep it to yourself!

Interpreter: To many he will say: Don't ask anything. Just listen. By merely listening, they understand; most of their doubts will be cleared. To that lady in the morning he said, just listen, don't ask any questions. That can be very effective, too. In the flow of the talk, many doubts will be cleared. He is sure of that.

V: Why is there such a divergence between different gurus, *rishis*, and realized yogis? Perhaps they are not realized?

M: No, this is to be explained as follows. Although consciousness is universal and the knowledge "you are," and whatever knowledge there is, is all common, its expression through the body and the mind is individualistic; there everything is different. Therefore, the path expounded by each sage will be different; it is bound to be so.

V: All those several paths lead to the...

M: They will lead to the same. Is it not that all paths lead to Delhi? The paths will be different, but the destination is the same. So you can't compare the path or what I am expounding with somebody else's.

V: In your method—may I call it method?—have you noticed any *siddhis*...

M: No. But that is my own doing, because of the commands of my guru. My guru told me, although you are realized, you will have to expound knowledge only. No *siddhi* powers for you. I was very eager...I thought, "I'll get certain powers, do miracles, remove the sickness of people." At first, I was thinking along those lines, as an initiate. But my guru told me, "Nothing of the sort for you. You have to expound knowledge only." There were to be no powers for me. And then he also told me, "You must repeat all these *bhajans* three or four times a day. You have to do it." He said, for the sake of all the ignorant people we have to do this.

I do not want to take you by the traditional, convention-al, tortuous ways. That is why my teachings are better liked by the foreigners, because none of this traditional, conven-tional thing is there.

V: The worshipping, the rituals, nothing is there.

M: That is the devotional path. But what I am giving you is *atma-yoga. I* am not "doing" *bhakti yoga*; that is, *bhajans*, etc.: It is happening, going on by itself! *Bhakti-yoga* means (a devotee) trying to link up with God. It is not only going on here; it is going on everywhere right from the ants. This means that everybody has that *bhakti*, even an ant wants to live, which is the same as *bhakti*. But that ant does not know it. Only a human form...

V: My question is, even a *jnani's bhajans* are devoted to some God, say Krishna, which takes for granted *saguna bhakti*. [*To the interpreter:*] Are you convinced by the answer? Then in turn you can convince me.

Interpreter: What has happened is this: as a *jnani* he would have remained unknown to the world. That is what his guru thought. So he told him, when Maharaj asked how he could repay this debt after he got realization, you cannot repay this anyway. But if at all you want to repay, you must do *bhajans* four times a day. Now the purpose of his guru's command was that when some *bhajan* goes on somewhere, people were alerted to the fact that this is a place where worship of God is taking place. So that is how people started coming here. Initially, they were mainly Indian people who were not primarily interested in knowing themselves, but who had faith in God. Those people came first, and subsequently others started flowing in, like Maurice Frydman. And thereafter that book [*referring to* I Am That] was published. Ultimately, you came to know of these teachings because of him. So the purpose of this *bhajan* was indirectly to let people know about him; otherwise, he would have remained absolutely unknown.

V: It may be correct, but there must be some more to it.

I: Because of this *bhajan*, people get elevated, don't they?

Normally, we practice whatever he tells you right at the moment. He wanted to elaborate a little on this point. Presently, when people are putting the same question again and again, he will not reply at all. He was trying to say, *bhajan* is going on right from the level of ants up to ours. Eventually, when you get true knowledge, ultimate knowledge, then only will you come to understand that *bhakti* and *jnana yoga* are one.

V: And one can get that ultimate knowledge either way?

I: Yes.

The questioner is giving details about a recent visitor to Maharaj, a prominent homeopathic physician from America, who has been asked to utilize his expertise in trying to alleviate Maharaj's illness.

M: Since I am abiding in the state which is prior to the *gunas*, the disease has had no effect on me during the past three months. I am not taking on any fear of that disease. I have voided these three *gunas* forever. And whatever is happening, is happening in the realm of these *gunas* only. The *gunas* are doing all this. I am the knower of the *gunas* and their realm, but I am not the *gunas*.

Now this disease which is said to be here, on what is that disease? Certainly not on me. That disease has occurred on that to which the name "birth" has been attached. Therefore, that which is born, is suffering from the disease, not me.

Then the next point is, what exactly is born? What is born are the three states: the waking state, the sleeping state and the knowledge "I am," this consciousness. The body and the vital breath would not be able to function if this consciousness were not present. So these are the three states which have been born. And these three states work through the three attributes (*gunas*). So these three states and the consequent three attributes, that bundle has been born and whatever happens, happens to that bundle only. I am not concerned with any of that.

I very clearly see that which has been born. And I also know that I am not that which is born. And that is why I am totally fearless. I am entirely without any reaction to a disease that would otherwise be traumatic.

Knowing that I am not that which is considered to be born, yet there is a little attachment to it. In what way? Attachment is to that with which I have been associated for a long time. There is that speck of attachment only because I have been attached to this body for eighty years. So I meet somebody from my hometown, whom I have known for a long time. He comes and goes away. I bid him goodbye. Now what happens? The fact that he is leaving or has left is not going to bother me. But when he leaves, there is that mere speck of attachment because something or somebody I have known for eighty years will be leaving. But that is all. There is not that firm attachment that usually occurs.

This consciousness, which is really what is born, mistakenly attaches itself to this body and thinks it is the body and works through the three *gunas*; that is the association. And it is that which is born. But I have nothing to do with this.

In the Gita, Lord Krishna tells Arjuna that you are not killing somebody, nor is anybody getting killed. The whole thing is an illusion.

The sweetness is the quality or nature of sugar; but that sweetness is there only so long as the sugar is present. Once the sugar has been consumed or thrown away, there is no more sweetness. So this knowledge "I am," this consciousness, this feeling or sense of Being, is the quintessence of the body. And if that body essence is gone, this feeling, the sense of Being, will also have gone. This sense of Being cannot remain without the body, just as sweetness cannot remain without the material, which is sugar.

V: What remains then?

M: What remains is the Original, which is unconditioned, without attributes, and without identity: that on which this temporary state of the consciousness and the three states and the three *gunas* have come and gone. It is called *Parabrahman*, the Absolute.

This is my basic teaching. Have you any questions on that?

V: I have no fundamental quarrel with it. The only thing I remember from carefully reading the books is that there is this tangle of memories that survives with the ordinary, unenlightened person. Is that completely undone in Maharaj's state?[2]

---

2   The question whether memories continue after disappearance of the being-ness frequently crops up because of its alleged relevance to the possibility of "rebirth." It is fueled particularly by two statements made in *I Am That* (Acorn Press, First American Edition, pp. 12 and 381) to the effect that certain memories are preserved, which may be taken as an affirmation that the personality continues after physical death. But, on the other hand, Maharaj states in the same breath, quite uneqivocally, that although the memories continue as images and concepts, they do not continue as belonging to the same person; they merely "supply the energy for *a new person.*" [*Italics by Editor*] Thus, the old personality does not undergo rebirth! Generally, Maharaj has an aversion to dealing with this issue. Partly, he feels this is like putting the cart before the horse; First understand the Self, by undoing all identification with the body-mind; then where is the question of "rebirth"? (See also p. 199 of the present work.).

M: If there is sugar or the juice of the sugar cane, then there can be sweetness. So if this physical material essence, which is the body, is not there, how can there be any memories? Even the awareness that you are alive, that you exist, the sense of beingness itself, is lost, just as the taste of sweetness is gone.

The lady's question was that after the body and the consciousness leave, there is something which is this *Parabrahman*. Then, how does one know this, whatever remains? How does one know that there is something? Look at it this way: Now there are twenty people in this room. All twenty people leave. Then what remains is that, but someone who has left cannot understand what it is. So in that *Parabrahman*, which is unconditioned, without attributes, without identity—the identity comes only when there is the knowledge "I am"—so if that itself is not there, who is there to ask? This is to be understood, not by "someone" (with a body-mind identity), but it must be experienced, and in such a manner that the experiencer and the experience are one. Therefore, you become the experience. Only that way you can know, and it is not the mind that knows it; the very mind has come subsequently, after true consciousness.

If someone asks, "What is this *Parabrahman* like?" the answer is it is like Bombay. Don't give me the geography of Bombay, don't tell me about the atmosphere in Bombay, but tell me what *is* Bombay? Is it possible to say? You cannot. So also there is nothing you can say, this is Bombay, or this is *Parabrahman*. If I ask you: Give me a handful of Bombay! you cannot oblige. Similarly, there is no giving or taking of *Parabrahman*: you can only *be* that. In fact, the concept or the thought "I am" itself is not there. The question was: Is it like sleep? No. Sleep, as I told you, is an attribute of that which has been born. So find out, what is it that has been born. Before the birth, even the thought that I exist is not there. Go home, ponder on it. Because it is something that must unfold itself. You can't use your brains or thought on it. The Absolute is not easy to get. All manifestation comes only from a speck of consciousness. [*Maharaj is addressing a particular lady in the audience*] Will you remember what I told you?

V: I will make an effort.

M: Remembering something, whatever it is, is itself an aspect of that consciousness which you are. If you don't have that consciousness, the question of remembering or even thinking does not arise. So the place to start is with this consciousness. And this consciousness can't be there without the body. This is the mystery that is to unfold.

The consciousness is there so long as the five elements are present. Now when what is called the great dissolution of the Universe,[3] of all the five elements, takes place, the consciousness also is finished. But the knower of the consciousness, the Absolute state, is unaffected. So I am always in that state and that is why there is no fear of anything. Even when everything was burning in the hole, and there was total destruction, I was merely watching. Just being in a state of witnessing, I was untouched by anything. So being that, what could affect me?

Secondly, whatever appears, really has no substance. It has only a temporary existence. And so long as the appearance is there, pain is also present. And when things disappear, pain is again absent. So only when form is present and the consciousness is there, you feel the pain or the misery. And when there is no form, there is no consciousness, and no feeling of any pain or anything.

V: Are there times in Maharaj's awareness when the form that we see is not in his field of awareness, so that he does not feel the pain of what is happening here?

---

3 According to Hindu cosmology, the existence of the Universe is cyclical in nature; it periodically undergoes total dissolution and re-creation.

M: So long as the consciousness is there, the pain is felt. But consciousness is the product of the food body, just as in the oil lamp when the oil is present there is a flame. Similarly, this body is like oil, and that flame is the knowledge "I am." Whatever you see, prior to all that, the knowledge "I am" must be there. And that itself contains the whole thing, your entire world of experience. So the greatest scene is that knowledge "I am" itself; that consciousness itself is the whole film in which everything is contained.

Therefore, the consciousness is there, the pain is felt, but I deny that as my real identity. How I got that real identity is through the guru, the guru's words, full faith in his words, and meditating on the consciousness, that knowledge; thereafter, I came to know that the usual saying that one is born in the world, is wrong. The fact is that my existence is forever. Ever there. I am not one of the world, but the world is in my consciousness. It was supposed that the body has appeared, has formed in this world. But when the truth came out, it was found that in a certain atom the entire Universe is contained. And what is that atom? It is the beingness, the knowledge "I am." That contains the whole Universe.

Because of your existence, because you know that you are, you know also that the world is. So this consciousness, because of which you experience the world, is not unimportant; in fact, it is very important. So why not stabilize there? Meditate on that consciousness itself, and find out how this "I-am-ness" has appeared. What was its cause? And from what did this consciousness develop? Try to find out, go right to the source!

July 4/5, 1980

4.

ONCE YOU KNOW YOU EXIST, YOU WANT TO REMAIN ETERNALLY

*M*AHARAJ: There are many persons who have a great attachment to their own individuality. They want first and foremost to remain as an individual and then search, for they are not prepared to lose that individuality. While retaining their identity, they want to find out what is the truth. But in this process, you must get rid of the identity itself. If you really find out what you are, you will see that you are not an individual, you are not a person, you are not a body. And people who cling to their body identity are not fit for this knowledge.

The names and forms that appear, with different colors and all that, their origin is water.[1] But nobody says I'm water, but they say I am the body. But if you see the origin of the body, then ultimately the body has appeared only from water. All these plants and everything, all names and forms, they appear from water only. But still people don't identify themselves with water; they say I am the body. The existence of heaven or hell, or whatever it is, is on this earth only. All names appertain to forms, and all forms appear from the earth and merge again into that. So they are con-

1 Cf. "From the waters everything is made, both what is manifest and what is Unmanifest. Therefore, all manifestation (*murti*) is water." — *Prasna Upanishad*, 1.4–5.

cepts, the existence of heaven and hell. Discoveries are
made by the scientists; they receive help from their own
consciousness, that knowledge "I am" itself. But what it is,
they don't know. They cannot get hold directly of whatever
they discover. Various books have been written, but ultimately Krishna, not a person, but consciousness in a form,
has written about itself, what it is. And that I find most
appropriate of all the existing scriptures.

VISITOR: You mean the Bhagavad Gita?

M: Yes, but I do not say Krishna is a person. It is consciousness in a particular form that authored the Bhagavad
Gita. The same consciousness is in you. And it is also this
consciousness that was there when you were a child, the
same as is present now also. As time passes, the consciousness remains what it is. I call it *bal-krishna*, the child-consciousness. You give attention to that; catch hold of it and
then you will know. That "I"-consciousness is the same in a
child as in an older person. If you consider the childhood of
present-day great people, great scholars, scientists, politi-
cians, what were they on the first day of their birth? At that
stage, the consciousness is present, but the "I"-conscious-
ness, that identification "I am," is not there; only *bal-
krishna*, child ignorance is there. The child does not know
that he exists. When he grows up, then only he comes to
know that he is; he recognizes the mother, and thereafter he
starts to gather so-called knowledge and becomes a great
scholar, a great man. But nobody knows what that child-
ignorance is. A *jnani* knows; that is why he becomes free.
He has no pride about Self-knowledge. The *jnani* knows the
origin of that consciousness.

    This atomic consciousness contains the whole Universe,
but yet he knows that he is not that consciousness. So in
that case, what pride can he have? He is the Absolute state,
in which the "I-am" consciousness is absent. If you meet

any *jnanis*, you will find it easy to recognize them, for they will not have any pride in their Self-knowledge since they have transcended that knowledge also. They say "I am not this knowledge or this consciousness."

The consciousness in the body leaves when death occurs. And what about that growth of worms created in the body? There is life in that, too. But the main consciousness has left. When the vital force leaves, the body falls.

For forty-two years I have been talking about this subject. When I met my guru, he told me to set aside all these various gods. He told me that my consciousness, because of which I experience the world, is prior to everything. That means I should reflect on this consciousness only, go to its source and find out what it is. The fact that I am experiencing that I am and the world is, is proof that when the dissolution of the universes[2] took place, I was unaffected. If I were to have died at that moment, I would not be experiencing this existence now.

So many great people have said something like Krishna, but when somebody speaks out, he should first know that he *is*; subsequently something occurs and he speaks. But prior to saying anything, that "I"-consciousness must be present. There was a time, in the Absolute state, when there was no beingness; and then beingness appeared and you said something. So whether it is true or false, prior to the appearance of beingness, you did not know that you were; so whatever you said after the beingness appeared, whether true or false, is also the same. The source of this beingness, of the knowledge "I am" that you have, is in the blade of grass and the grain of rice.

Those people who expound knowledge believe that the world is first and they were born in it afterwards. So long as this conviction is there, they cannot expound knowledge; they don't know better. When the "I"-consciousness is

---

2 See footnote on p. 37

there, then only the words come out. Prior to the appearance of that consciousness, are there any words? No, you were unknowing of your own existence. Now the first thing you come to know is that you are. And then you say something that occurs to you, don't you? So whatever you say, whether it is the truth or not, what is the basis for it?

When the beingness is not there, there are no words. Once the beingness appears, whatever occurs is taught to the "disciples" and is promulgated as "religion." But they are only concepts. That you exist, how do you come to know it first? Because of what? Now at this moment you come to know that you are. How do you know?

V: I don't know. It is just that this sense is with me, that is all. I can't trace its source.

M: When you know the source of this beingness or "I"-consciousness—that is liberation. Then you become free. Not until then.

V: All I know at this stage, from following the practice Maharaj recommends, is that the more I dwell in that the happier I am and the less concerned I am with my status in the world.

M: Whatever you are saying is just a saying in this world. Prior to the appearance of beingness, if you had known about your existence, eternal and absolute, knowingly would you have entered this form, this body? Now what has happened is that you did not know you were there, initially. Only when you became a two or three-year old child you started knowing that you exist. So whatever had happened until then, nine months in the womb and one or two years afterwards, is pure ignorance. Unknowingly, all this has happened. So the question is, prior to entering the womb, knowingly would you have done it?

V: Well, it depends upon what sort of advertisement I saw about the world. Knowing what I do now, I don't think that I would have wanted to.

M: Upon a person's death, the first stage is that he does not know that he *is*, beingness has left. The consciousness, the "I-am-ness," is not there. Then the doctor comes and confirms it, and the body goes for cremation. And because of that which caused the "I-am" knowledge to be present, the body material is there but that "I-am" knowledge is now absent. That "I"-consciousness is not there in the body, so whether you bury or cremate it, cut it into pieces, whatever you do, does it matter? There is nobody to protest.

I am giving you some homework now. Whatever you have heard, when you go home, ponder on this subject and write down some points. If you have any questions, you may ask them the next day.

Interpreter: Many of the disciples write to Maharaj and say "I am separated from you, being in the West and you are here; I don't have money to come, but I don't feel you are not here. You are here, you and me are one." That sort of letters he is getting. They are also experiencing the oneness, the non-dual state.

V: They don't go beyond that.

M: But they cannot transcend, they cannot go beyond that. But still they feel they should come here, although there is oneness. I tell them when they come here, your consciousness is mySelf. So long as you have the conviction that you are a man or a woman, then you miss me. But if you take yourself as the consciousness, then I am always with you— that I call "marriage." You want to get married with me? Then have these convictions.

Now I am going again to the source. *Janmarlana* means "birth-marriage." Who are the two parties that are getting married at the source? *Janmarlana*, the birth-marriage or the union of two entities: one is called the mother, but it is fluid power. And the other is called the father, who is also fluid power when they unite. That is birth.

This is my spirituality, my study of spirituality; this is what I have been doing all these years. And I have come to the stage to know that I am that principle which was unaffected by the dissolution of the universes.[3] Those are my convictions. I am telling you from my experience that I did not undergo any pain when the whole Universe was on fire, was being destroyed. I was unaffected. Is it true or false?

V: Of Maharaj's experience?

M: Yes.

V: I believe it, that it is true.

M: That is why that as far as I am concerned, heaven and hell do not exist. There are other people who believe in those and they may experience that sort of thing, but for me they don't exist.

INTERPRETER: For the past forty-two years he has been talking; now he says that gives him pain because of his ill health. He tells people, especially foreigners who come here, to gather whatever knowledge they can in a short time.

M: Jnaneshwar, a great sage, said, I don't tell a lie; whatever exists has no substance, it is unreal.[4] The present moment is unreal.

---

3 See footnote on p. 37
4 CF"From the beginning not a thing is."— Hui–neng, the Sixth Patriarch of Chinese Zen Buddhism.

Prior to the appearance of beingness, I did not exist. So what was there? Now you say you exist. So I am going to talk on this subject. What is this existence, or is it non-existence? You tell me sixty or a hundred years back, I was not there. So what existed then? What was there a hundred years back? Whatever you reply, is it true or false?

V: I believe it is true. It is just an honest statement of my knowledge. I don't know, I have no memory of it.

M: So whatever you were saying you were not, that is the real existence. That is true, and whatever you say that you are now is false; that is the truth because it is eternal. That is the state in which the beingness is absent, the eternal state. And because it is eternal, it is the truth. Now with your "I-am-ness," which is time-bound, it is not eternal; that is why it is untruth—eternal existence of the untruth. The principle which now replies I don't know what was there a hundred years back, the same principle also says that it was unaffected when the whole universe was destroyed.

If you have full faith in the guru, it means you have his grace. consciousness or the beingness itself is the love; it is formless. And it wants to exist all the time. That itself is love. That love wants to *be*. So all your efforts are for that, to sustain that. And that is of supreme importance, because it contains the whole world. Because of that, you experience the world. The world is in that consciousness.

Since you are the *Brahman*, you lose your identification with the body; you are no longer a human being as you identity yourself with the *Brahman*. And that is like a raw mango, which slowly becomes a ripe one; in that state you will see that you are not even the *Brahman* but the *Parabrahman*, the witness of that *Brahman*.

It is essential to understand the working of this body and life force—that is, the psychosomatic process. One must understand it in order to apperceive that the knower is totally apart from this psychosomatic mechanism; he merely witnesses. Now in this body, the life force is a concept, but conceptually there are four parts. The ones we normally know and understand are the *madhyama* and *vaikhari*. *Madhyama* is the thought that comes and gets expressed by the word but underneath that are *para* and *pashyanti*; they underlie and start the whole process. When the words have come out spontaneously through the life force, the breath, they are known as Vedas. When a stage is reached where the Vedas are no longer able to explain what happens, we call it Vedanta, which means the end of the Vedas. But the knower of this is totally separate and not concerned with the body. That is what is to be thoroughly understood.

I: The disease that he has is of the body and the (vital) breath. Earlier he said, he has passed it on, whatever that disease is, to the beingness. So let the beingness be concerned with it! If the beingness wants to accentuate it, let it do so. If it wants to hold it in abeyance, it can do so. In any case he is merely the witness, and he has passed it on to the beingness on which the disease has really come; that is, the body and the beingness. The life force is the working principle in this apparatus.

M: Whatever is dependent on the life force, including the Veda, exists only so long as the body and the breath last, and the consciousness. When that which is time-bound disappears, then everything else also disappears. Even the Veda disappears. But the knower of this is timeless, spaceless, and is not concerned with what happens to the body, vital breath and consciousness.

When the breath disappears, this apparatus is also useless. And the one who knows this will not identify himself with the psychosomatic process or the apparatus. If he knows this intuitively and very clearly, he can be said to have had *jnana*. The knower has been given various names—*atman, paramatman*, Ishwara, God. Names have been given only for the purpose of communication. Unless the principle or concept is given a name, there cannot be any communication. So it must be kept in mind that that which is called *atman* is not a thing with a shape or form.

Yesterday we discussed how one is likely to mistake the name for the thing. That is to be avoided, and that is why if someone asks what is the *paramatman* like, what is the Absolute like, then you may say it is like Bombay. That is merely a name given, you cannot give me a part of Bombay if I asked for it. But one should not be involved with the name to the extent that one forgets the substance. Various names have been given to that Absolute state, but it must be understood that it is unconditioned, has no attributes and possesses no identity.

Any spiritual practice anyone may do is really based only on the working principle, which is the vital breath, and will therefore last only so long as that breath lasts. Whatever knowledge you have acquired of any kind, material or spiritual, is based only on this consciousness or breath. Other than that, there is no knowledge which anyone in the manifest world can acquire. It is based on this and, therefore, inherently strictly limited. So one may think he is doing this practice on the *atman*, but he is not actually doing it on the *atman*; *atman* is quite separate altogether. He is doing it only from the point of view of the life force. Because of this practice, when the life force is tired, it wants rest. And when you rest, it may go into a state of *samadhi*. But whatever experience you may have, even in *samadhi*, is also not timeless; it is subject to time and the one who experiences is different from the experience itself. The experiencer[5] is totally apart. It is up to us to understand the experience and not get involved in it.

---

5 To be understood here as the Ultimate Experiencer, not the limited experiencer in the form of the psychosomatic organism.

What goes on in the world is based on this life force only. And the life force acts through the words. The entire action in the world is based on this, but the *atman*, the experiencer or the witness is totally apart. And, to repeat, the witness is like Bombay. No action can be attributed to the one who is the witness only. Can Bombay do anything? Any action will last only so long as the life force is there.

One has landed himself in bondage by identifying with a name and form. But one is really that thing which is timeless, spaceless and without identity. Now when we seek truth, we seek truth with a form and that is where the trouble arises. There is name and form and action. The moment the life force disappears, there is no name, no form, no acquisition, no hopes, ambition—nothing.

From the beginning of the life force to the end of it, or when the life force is tired, when it goes into rest, it is timebound. The arising of the three states (waking, sleep and knowingness) is based on this life force which has appeared. It is not the result of anyone's desire, neither yours nor mine; it is a spontaneous happening. Whatever practice one does is done through the instrument of the life force and is therefore time-bound. So one must not be mistaken to think that what one is doing is through the *atman*. Whatever bondage one thinks one has is also based on these concepts, which are built up because of the life force, and they are all time-bound.

Now what is this bondage, why have we got into it? It is because the mind flows out into words—hence this *madhyama* and *vaikhari* (the earlier two stages, *para* and *pashyanti* are imperceptible). *Madhyama* is the mind and *vaikhari* is the words coming out. And through this, the thoughts and the words, we have mistaken our identity as "me" and "mine," whereas whatever takes place is independent of the one who witnesses and is based entirely on the life force. Would you please understand very clearly that this life force has mistakenly identified itself with the body and the thoughts and the words, and then considers itself to be guilty of something or that is has acquired merit by certain actions, whereas everything takes place independently merely through the action of the life force. If this is clearly understood then there is no question of either bondage or acquisition of any merit. Is there any God? With the end of the life force, there is no movement, no thought, no word, no waxing or waning.

V: Does the physical death means the end of the life force? If yes, is there no truth in the theory of rebirth?

M: The four kinds of speech, *para*, *pashyanti*, *madhyama* and *vaikhari*, are the names of the vital breath. Ordinarily, an individual is not aware of *para* and *pashyanti*. These two are too subtle, too basic and too deep for him to understand. So he starts working on the third one, *madhayma*, which is also identified with the mind and comes out with words, and the fourth stage which is called *vaikhari*. Now on this level of two minds, two kinds of speech, every ignorant individual works. And he has his own image made out of that *madhyama*, which is mind. If he is ignorant and has not understood this secret of the Universe, he will certainly talk about rebirth, birth and other ideas, concepts with which he has identified himself. Therefore, all these ideas and concepts of rebirth are for the ignorant. Otherwise, there is nothing.

V: Is the science of astrology also in the field of mind that is *madhyama*, this third type of speech?

M: Remember that *madhyama* is the name given to the mind, and when there is no vital breath, where is astrology, where is the future, where is the past, for any *prani*, any living being? One identifies with all the Vedas, all the activities, all that is happening in the world, so long as he has not understood the vital breath, whose language is all the four languages. You should understand all the kinds of speech that flow through the vital breath, *prana*. So long as you do not recognize this, you are bound to take as absolutely certain whatever mind—that is, *madhyama*—tells you. Those concepts which the mind has given you will be final for you; thus, there will be heaven and hell and all kinds of merit and demerit. On the other hand, once the vital breath is understood, the one who observes, the witness, is absolutely different, absolutely separate from all these activities that are going on in the world.

V: What is the difference after death between a person who has understood during his lifetime and a person who has not understood?

M: The man who has understood this vital breath is beyond any mental concept, and the one who has not understood is a slave to his thoughts, which are the emanations of the mind.

V: No, but his question was about after death!

M: What do you call death? Now these ingredients have finished burning. They are finished! Does that mean they are dead? When anything becomes invisible, you call it death. It is not that. When something becomes visible, you call it birth.

V: What is the point of assuming a human body?

I: He will not go over these elementary points again in these discussions. Now there are breezes and winds and storms coming over Bombay. Is Bombay suffering or enjoying anything? So also are *paramatman* and *atman*; they are nothing but to be understood.

V: But if after death, the state of the man of knowledge and the man who has not understood are the same, what is the point of trying to become a man of knowledge?

M: Who will say of the qualityless and attributeless *Parabrahman* that he is attributeless after death? Only one who understands while living that he is *nirguna*—qualityless, attributeless—he alone will say it. He does not know whether he is or he is not. Non-beingness or beingness have absolutely no effect on him. That is *nirguna*, that is *Parabrahman*. Bombay itself does not know that it exists or does not exist. Does the soul, *atman*, go to hell or heaven? People say, I have a serious illness, but what am I experiencing? I am experiencing only the vital breath. The vital breath sets and the beingness goes, but I am not affected.

I am asked the question: Can we say that you and I are identical? So I say, show me the sample of what you are and show me the sample of what I am, then I can tell you whether we are the same.

V: But I am sure that all his disciples would like him to continue the manifestation. If a deep wish comes from his disciples, would he respond?

M: What is the need of responding? The one who has deep faith, according to that he will experience.

The experience of this world has come over us due to somebody enjoying ecstasy, and from the fluid of our parents' ecstasies have sprung all our woes and miseries.

V: Does he mean that the two always go together? Is it necessary that in the mind both happiness and unhappiness ever coexist?

M: All these concepts are the result of not understanding your nature. Because you have not understood what you are, misery is the result.

V: Does Maharaj look after his family and other things responsibly?

I: Yes, and more than that.

V: Talking of the vital force, the two aspects of it that we are commonly conscious of are our thoughts and the manifest of thoughts as words. What are the other two aspects of the life force? Do we have to be aware of them in the course of our *sadhana*?

M: That you are aware of your existence, your beingness, is *para* and *pashyanti*—two kinds of expression or speech that I talked about. Awareness of your existence is to be aware of these two kinds of speech. Their meaning is that you are in the three stages, waking, sleep and knowingness. The next two kinds of speech are what you performed in the world, your business, how you carried it out with your mind and its activities.

These four types of speech can always be distinguished in the following way: The first one, *para*, corresponds to your original state when you don't even know you exist. Then comes this feeling that you are about to become conscious. That is still *para*, but it is followed by *pashyanti*, which is this consciousness—when you say, yes, I am alive, I am awake, I exist. Once having this consciousness that you exist, the behavior in the world corresponds with the two final aspects of the vital force. At this stage, the thought comes, the mind starts working (*madhyama*) and the words start flowing through the mind (*vaikhari*).

To recapitulate: First, I am not even conscious; I do not know that I exist, then this consciousness forces itself on that state of unawareness to an extent that we begin to feel that we are conscious. Finally, it forces itself into full consciousness, and I know that I exist, I am there. And that becomes a concept, from which starts the entire world of troubles. In that original state when you are not aware, there is no trouble of any kind. But once this consciousness makes its presence felt, all the trouble starts. This is not mine, I know this is not mine, but it is forced upon me, and then also I begin to say that it is "me"—this is the way that identification takes place.

Earlier, the question arose, when I said consciousness, did I mean the body? I said, no, not the body. For the consciousness to appear, it needs a body, it needs a vehicle, and the body is the food for this consciousness. Without food, the body cannot exist, and consciousness cannot exist without the body. So this body is the food for consciousness to exist. If the body disappears, the food disappears, and then the consciousness will also disappear. Then also it may be asked: Is there any difference between what is termed *atman* or the self and this consciousness? It is the same thing, but different words are used in different contexts; the content is basically the same. I use the word "taste," the essence of the body; the taste of that essence is this beingness, of being alive, and wanting to be alive. One loves the state of being alive and wants to perpetuate it as long as possible. So the love for this consciousness is this taste.

V: I have one other question. I heard through the translation of what was being said this morning that most of the spiritual practices that we do in a kind of motivated way are attempts to manipulate ourselves. It is just really the play of the life force.

M: So do they have any value, is that what you mean to ask?

V: No, no. My question is, if this is what we do, how is it that the witness state, which seems to be the core of Maharaj's communication to us, can arise at all in the midst of all these attempts?

M: Although time-bound, the practice will unfold itself in the consciousness. The only important thing is its unfoldment. This will happen when through meditation we give it our fullest attention; then, the consciousness which has come upon us and is pure ignorance, will itself show you your true nature. There is no question of going anywhere, arriving anywhere, or doing anything; you are there already.

One has to work in the world; naturally, carry on your worldly affairs, but understand that that which has come about by itself—that is, this body, mind and consciousness—has appeared in spite of the fact that nobody has asked for it. I did not ask for it; it has come upon me in my original state which is timeless, spaceless, and without attributes. So that whatever has happened is doing this business in the world. The life force and the mind are operating, but the mind will tempt you to believe that it is "you." Therefore, understand always that you are the timeless, spaceless witness. And even if the mind tells you that you are the one who is acting, don't believe the mind. Always keep your identity separate from that which is doing the working, thinking and talking. That which has happened—that is, the apparatus which is functioning—has come upon your original essence, but you are not that apparatus. This is to be firmly kept in mind.

Every sentient being has a guru within himself. Unless the guru were present, the being would not have come about. The beingness itself is the guru.

With respect to the four kinds of speech, they are the result of the vital force. Whenever the vital force is present, there is the *atman*, and vice-versa. When the force leaves the body, all the four kinds of speech also go, and the *atman*, of course, is not felt. "I"-consciousness, beingness and all activities happen only because of the vital force. Thus, when this force leaves the body and the "I"-consciousness is no more there, the body falls. Then, I am asking you, who is there?

V: It is nameless. I don't know who is there; it has no name.

M: The existence of the vital force and the "I"-conscious-ness have the experience of your existence. That is why and how you know that you are; without them you could not know about your own existence.

[*To a new visitor:*] Do you have any guru? You are prac-ticing yoga. What were you trying to unite, what with what? What were the two entities?

V: To remove the ego.

M: At the moment, you just listen to whatever talks go on here; so sit in the back somewhere. If you like it, you can stay; otherwise, you need not come. But don't ask any ques-tions. Just listen to the questions and the replies. As a new-comer, you want to ask any questions? You think you don't know; that is correct. And whatever you think you know, that is not correct. Whatever you understand is not correct. And whatever you do not understand is correct. The former has a beginning and an end. Whatever you do not under-stand has no beginning and so no end.

V: The mind has to be still, because its movement is to cre-ate a disturbance.

M: You said, you are not the mind. So whether the mind is quiet or unsteady, how are you concerned? You are not the mind. Whatever you don't know, you are. So do you feel the need to sit here any longer?

What I meant is, if you really understand what was said, there is no need to attend. If you understood, once and for all, you can go.

V: I think, what a lot of us feel is that some of us are good at reading books, and others are not so good at that. And it is only too easy to spout back the verbal input we get. But there is so much more that happens when we are in Maharaj's company, whether it is his physical presence or even only when reading the books. And I think that is what draws us so strongly to be with him. Because it is as if the need for all the talk at times just gets undone and that presence makes itself felt.

M: After having acquired this "I"-consciousness as a child, whatever impressions you gathered subsequently, on that basis only you talk. So that talk is bound to have limited value; it is only objective knowledge.[6]

V: The only purpose in any communication from Maharaj is to serve our freedom from all that. Sometimes, concepts need to be clarified, but that is the only purpose. But I feel a greater purpose for me in coming here is to drop a lifetime of concern with concepts.

M: Childhood itself is a cheat. There is no truth in that. Supporting all this, whatever your body form—and your body form went on changing—your objective knowledge also continued to change; ultimately, you grow old. Whatever happens, it is all like a dream; it has no substance. And supporting this entire dream, this untruth, is that child; it all began there. As a child, you began gathering knowledge and when you became very old, you forgot everything. So all that objective knowledge was of no use. Now, I am asking, what are you at the moment? Whatever you have gathered as your identity or your form, you are in the process of losing. So what then is your real identity?

Suppose somebody becomes very old, say one hundred

---

6 That is, knowledge of "objects" from a subject's point of view, and therefore fragmentary, ultimately restricted to name and form.

twenty-five years, and then becomes very weak, and ultimately is about to die. Now why is it said that that person
is dead? Because of what?

V: Objectively, it is very clear to me when a person is dead;
the vital breath just leaves and the body is merely a heap of
decaying cells after that.

M: When the childhood gets exhausted or extinguished,
you call him dead. Because the childhood was originally
there, the person was living.

V: Does Maharaj mean life begins and ends with a childish
state of mind? I take it that with childhood the body is set
into motion. And in a sense, death is the end of the motion
that was initiated at birth.

M: Why is it called childhood, what is that entity, and how
does that name "childhood" first appear? Try to understand
that. What is the principle called "childhood"?

V: Consciousness is very rudimentary in a child. There is as
yet no sense of his independent existence, no sense of I am
this or I am that—a kind of randomness.

M: In a raw fruit, is there sweetness?

V: No.

M: Ultimately, that sweetness comes, does it not? Where
does it come from?

V: From the biochemical changes that occur when the fruit
ripens.

M: When you will understand what this childhood is, then that is liberation. Paradoxically, you will realize that you are already liberated. You must try to understand your "I"-consciousness or beingness. With that you can obtain a lot of objective knowledge and try to control the world. And if you don't understand this consciousness itself, then you are in bondage. You may do anything in the world, but ultimately you are in shackles. The consciousness, the child-consciousness, has to know the consciousness. It has to know itself. That is the only way. If you live for a thousand years, whatever identity you will have from time to time, nothing will remain the same. You will not have any permanent identity for yourself even with such a long life span.

Everything is contained within the knowledge that you are a child, and all that will finally go. So your whole identity will disappear, including even that child identity, eventually.

This childhood, and this child-consciousness, is it true? One who has recognized the fact that it is false, what will you say about that man?

The one who has understood this, becomes in terms of the Vedas, *nirguna*, *nirvana*. *Nirvana* means no sample. *Nirguna* means beyond consciousness. So the activities of that, *nirguna* or *nirvana*, are like this city of Bombay. What are its activities? One who has understood this truth and has transcended it, his activities are like the city of Bombay.

V: I think the activities are much greater from the city of Bombay and certainly spread much further.

M: What I mean by the city of Bombay is without this land, without the earth portion. Because you cannot say exactly what this Bombay city is.

V: I think there are much better metaphors for it.

M: Small and big you can compare, when there is something as a standard. But if what is to be designated as big or small is the only existing entity, how can you compare? If you cannot show something as smaller, then you cannot present something as large; the whole thing is relative.

V: But we do that all the time.

M: For your worldly activities, in the objective world, yes, you use those terms, like in a dream. So all those activities are like those in the dream, the behavior in the dream state. Like that, all the activities happen.

V: For some of us, life creates incredibly complicated and superficially appealing dreams. The great challenge is to accept these as dreams and see through the bondage they represent to us—their implications for name and fame and our inability to let go of all that.

M: Now this consciousness...as it began with your consciousness as a child, when that "I"-consciousness first appeared...because of its appearance, you can say that somebody is very great. But suppose that this consciousness had not appeared at all, could you then have detected the greatness of somebody?

V: I would not have known, I would be non-conscious.

M: So it means that in the absence of that child-consciousness, you cannot detect greatness, does it not?

V: The funny thing about our first impressions of self-awareness as a child is the painful memories that usually bring you to that rather than all the happy playful times, when there was just no need and you were not thrown back on yourself.

M: So remembering childhood means painful experiences, according to you?

V: Well, that is the first time that self-awareness arises, when you are hurt, rejected, beaten up by your friends, when your mother spanks you, when your mother or father neglects your need for love.

M: Childhood itself is painful. Without that childhood, there is no experience of pain, is there? Very straight, very simple to understand. One who has not experienced childhood, will he have any experience of pain? It all starts with that.

V: I don't think adulthood is very much better, on its own terms.

M: We are talking about the beginning of everything. It all began with childhood. Now that childhood is also a concept, an idea. So if you understand that, you transcend at once all concepts. That is why it is imperative to understand childhood.

What is the function of childhood? Its function is for you to know that you exist. That is all it has done. Prior to that, you had no experience of the "I"-consciousness. My statement, and that of my guru, is that childhood is a cheat, it is false. The knowledge "I am" itself is a cheat. When the beingness appears, that love for existence is the result of the primary illusion, that *maya*. Once you come to know that you exist, you feel like enduring eternally. You always want to be, to exist, to survive. And so the struggle begins. All because of that *maya*.

I: The doctor has told him not to talk.

V: How could any doctor tell Maharaj not to talk? That is the very reason for his being with us.

I: He says, the doctor who examined him and found out what is wrong with him, has advised him not to talk.

V: That is standard advice. Here you have the supreme doctor of life and death, and his medicine comes through his words.

July 5/6, 1980

5.

THE GREATEST MIRACLE IS THE NEWS "I AM"

*M*AHARAJ: Whatever appears has really no existence. And whatever has not appeared also drops away; what remains is That, the Absolute. "That" is like Bombay.

VISITOR: Bombay certainly seems to be appearing at the moment. We should sell him another city.

M: But I normally ask you this kind of question; whether Bombay sleeps, whether it wakes up in the morning, whether it is worried, whether is has pain and pleasure. I do not refer to the people of Bombay, nor to the land, but to that which remains.

Now you know that you are. Prior to this moment, did you have this knowledge that you exist? This consciousness, beingness, which you are experiencing now, was it there earlier?

V: It has been, on and off.

M: This confidence that you are, the knowledge of your existence, was it there earlier?

V: When I do what Maharaj tells me, it is very clear. It is

still in an infantile stage, but my sense of "me" is completely undone, and there arises great happiness, peace and clarity; but it comes and goes, and I forget.

M: Its inherent nature is time-bound. It has appeared as childhood and it is there now; but it wasn't there some years back. So you cannot possibly say that it is the Eternal. So don't believe that it is true.[1] And so long as you are having this "I"-consciousness, you will be trying to acquire things; so long as you know that you are, the things that you possess have an emotional significance to you. Now there is the fact that your "I"-consciousness itself is time-bound. So when this dissolves, what is the value of all those things which you possessed?

V: Nil.

M: As long as you have not understood this child-consciousness, you'll get involved in the world and its activities. Therefore, the real liberation is only when you understand that child-consciousness. Do you agree?

V: I do agree.

M: During your entire lifetime, you do not have any permanent identity. Whatever you consider yourself to be changes from moment to moment. Nothing is constant.

V: And what you think you are going to become changes too, with time, in spite of yourself.

M: That change is also made possible by the child-consciousness. Because of that, all these changes take place. That is why you must grasp this principle.

---

1 On the basis that a transitory appearance cannot be the real.

If you really want to understand this, you must give up your identification with the body. By all means, make use of the body, but don't consider yourself to be the body while acting in this world. Identify yourself with the consciousness, which dwells in the body; with that identity, you should act in the world. Will it be possible?

So long as you identify yourself as the body, your experience of pain and sorrow will increase day by day. That is why you must give up this identification, and you should take yourself as the consciousness. If you take yourself as the body, it means you have forgotten your true Self, which is the *atman*. And sorrow results for the one who forgets himself. When the body falls, the principle which always remains is You. If you identify yourself with the body, you will feel that you are dying, but in reality there is no death because you are not the body. Let the body be there or not be there, your existence is always there; it is eternal.

Now who or what has heard my talk? It is not the ear, not the physical body, but that knowledge which is in the body; that has heard me. So identify yourself with that knowledge, that consciousness. Whatever happiness we enjoy in this world is only imaginary. The real happiness is to know your existence, which is apart from the body. You should never forget the real identity that you possess. Consider a patient on his deathbed, certain to die. Now when he first comes to know of his disease, say cancer, he gets such a shock that it is permanently engraved in his memory. Like that, you should never forget your true nature—the true identity I have told you about.

A patient who is suffering from cancer is, as it were, all the time silently chanting "I'm dying from cancer"; and that chant proceeds without any efforts. Similarly, in your case: Take up that chant "I am consciousness." That chant, too, should go on without any effort. One who is constantly awake in his true nature—having this knowledge about him-self—is liberated.

A patient suffering from terminal cancer always remembers his state and ultimately undergoes that very end; so much is certain. Similarly, one who remembers that he is the knowledge, that he is the consciousness, has that end, he becomes the *Parabrahman*.

So if you are about to photograph this land, I would say, no don't photograph...take a photograph of it but without land. Whatever is Bombay, take a photograph of that and show me. Can you?

V: I could not do it.

M: So that is like photographing yourself without the body. You are that, like Bombay. Remembering that you are the consciousness should be without any effort. When you say "I," don't refer to this body's "I," but to that "I" which represents this consciousness. The consciousness is "I," and make use of this knowledge when you act.

The pleasure or happiness that you have had, is it through the words that you have heard or because you have had a glimpse of your *atman*?

V: I have been studying a lot all along in doing the *sadhana*. Since I met Maharaj, things are becoming clarified and also I am getting confirmation of what I have learned.

M: What should be your ultimate conclusion after reading a lot, doing *sadhana* and listening to these talks? It is that the hearer, the knower, is not concerned with the *upadhi*—that is, the body, mind and consciousness—and that he is separate from this *upadhi* that has come upon him.

V: Does that mean *sakshivan*, witness-consciousness?

M: You use that word *sakshivan*, but what do you really mean by it? That there is sentience, through which you see what is happening. But other than that, is anything needed for witnessing to take place? The sun has arisen, and there is daylight. Have you put yourself out to do any witnessing? Or do you see effortlessly; therefore, witnessing simply takes place. There is nothing that what you call the "witness" has to do; witnessing happens purely by itself.

This knowledge "I am" has dawned on you. Since then, whatever other knowledge you have acquired, whatever experiences you have had, whatever you have seen of the world, has all been witnessed. But that one to whom the witnessing takes place is entirely separate from that which is witnessed. In this witnessing, in these experiences, you have assumed that you are the body, and you are involved in it. Therefore, you get the reactions of whatever you have seen and witnessed only through this identification with the body. But actually, you are not concerned with that which makes your seeing possible and that which has been seen. You are apart from either of them.

V: Living the worldly life and being a person of the *grihastha ashrama*,[2] drudging, working, sleeping, laughing, mixing with people of all nationalities, is it possible just to *be*, and not identify oneself entirely with the body?

M: Show me a sample of that which you think is identifying itself with the body.

V: Generally, one identifies oneself with the body. One should not do so. You are not body, consciousness or *buddhi*. You are something different. "I" is something different. But you do identify living in this world. Is it possible not to identify completely?

---

2 Householder stage of life. In the Hindu tradition, four successive *asramas* or stages of life are prescribed for spiritual perfection: *brahmacharya* (celibate disciple), *grihastha* (householder and family man), *vanaprastha* (forest dweller) and *sannyasa* (wandering monk, renunciant).

INTERPRETER: That question has been conveyed. But Maharaj is asking: "What is this 'I' that cannot keep away from identifying with....?"

V: The same "I" of which Maharaj talks.

M: Why is there any relationship between you and what goes on in the world? How does the relationship between the body and the world arise?

V: Because the "I" is encased in the body. And it is the body that keeps coming in contact with material beings, other bodies, animate and inanimate.

M: You think it is the body that is coming in contact. If that consciousness had not been there, how could the body have come in contact with the rest of the world? What actually is it that comes in contact with the world?

V: The "I" comes in contact with the world through the body.

M: Whatever the *madhyama* is, if that consciousness were not there, where is the question of either the mind medium or that with which the medium comes into contact? If the consciousness were not there, then does the body exist or even the world exist?

V: That is very correct.

M: Then consider this beingness or consciousness as the supreme God and let go(d). And even then, you as the knower of this are separate from the consciousness and the body.

V: I understand.

M: That which you have understood can work no more mischief on you, then. Is it not so? [*laughter*]

V: I have understood with my *buddhi*.

M: Which means that you can only use the instrument of the intellect to understand. But what is prior to the intellect?

V: The *atman*.

M: You understand the *atman*. Therefore, that which understands the *atman* must be prior to even the *atman*.

V: That means *buddhi*.

M: *Atman* is prior to *buddhi*, and you understand *buddhi* and also that *atman* is prior to *buddhi*.

V: I understand *atman* with *buddhi*; my *buddhi* tells me that there is *atman*. I want to understand *atma-jnana*. With *buddhi-jnana* came *atma-jnana*. I want the *atma-jnana*, not *buddhi-jnana*.

M: There should be no confusion. Understand a simple fact and that is that any kind of experience can only come upon the consciousness that is there. And you are separate from both that consciousness and the experiences which come on that consciousness.

Unless there is consciousness, call it *buddhi*, mind or whatever, can anything be there? The answer is obviously, no. Thus, in that consciousness I can see my body and the world; and it is basically only on that consciousness that any movement or experience can take place.

V: So that consciousness has the power to think? Or to feel?

M: On that consciousness, something happens. Whatever

movement, thought, or experience there is can occur only on this consciousness. And you are prior to this consciousness; therefore you are neither the consciousness—that is, the instrument—nor any thought or experience, or whatever it is that is happening on that instrument. You are totally apart from it. Now stick to that.

V: Stick to what?

M: To the fact that you are apart from it.

V: And you are That. That I know. But oftentimes, one cannot forget that one is in the body.

M: Remember that this body is made of the five elements; it is a material body—I call it food-body—and in that is this consciousness because of which the body possesses its sentience, enabling the senses to function. For the senses in the body operate only thanks to the consciousness. And you are separate from this body and the consciousness. That is the only thing to remember.

All you have is the vital breath, the life force. And part of the *prana* is the *atman*. Other than that, what have you got? I keep coming back to the same thing. Other than that, there is absolutely nothing.

[*Maharaj is commenting on "X," who is having a lot of troubles.*] All these difficulties that come and go should be merely watched like something in a play. When one scene is finished, another scene takes place, going on like an act. Then, the entire act and the entire play, does it take place anywhere but in yourself? If she did not have this consciousness, would she be aware of this play that is going on? So ultimately, whatever the play, whatever scenes and acts that take place, they are merely movements in her own consciousness.

[*The lady has been urging Maharaj to take care of himself.*] Who is to take care of what? I know what has come upon my original state, and there is nothing to take care of that. It is a happening that has come and will take care of itself. And whatever has happened, I have not been affected. So, again, who is to take care of what? I am not concerned with taking care of anything. The world has been in existence for millions of years. There have been thousands of avatars and great men, and important personalities. Has a single one of them been able to do anything to change the course of events in the world?

Whatever has come upon this original state is time-bound, but the original state is timeless and spaceless. And that is one whole, a Wholeness. Not really one, because if you say "one," there are immediately two.

V: Is what Ramakrishna said and what Maharaj is saying the same thing?

M: I have already told you, the basic essence is only whole. All these differences are subsequent; they are to the concepts. So basically, when in the Wholeness, how can there be sin or merit, or *any* kind of duality?

There is something by which you are able to say that you understand. And you are separate from that. What you think you have understood is only a movement in your consciousness. And you are separate from that consciousness. So as far as you are concerned, there is no question of understanding or not understanding.

V: We always think when we have a mental grasp of someone's teaching that *ipso facto* we have realized that teaching. But we have not at all, we are essentially the same person, suffering in the same way.

M: How did that original creation take place of the body as infant? And even prior to its birth: How did the conception happen? How did the infant come into being, without it asking for it? Understand that. Understand thoroughly that drop of stuff which eventually has developed into a body, and then you will understand the whole mystery that you are not that. This body that is now occupying a certain space, how much space did it occupy upon its conception? And what was it then? If you understand that, you will understand the mystery of the Self.

You base yourself on the body that you are now, and don't understand its root. That is why we think we are this body. And for that, you must do meditation. What is meditation? Meditation is not this body-mind meditating as an individual, but it is this knowledge "I am," this consciousness, meditating on itself. Then the consciousness will unfold its own beginning.

Identification is with what? With this body that is now. But does it understand its origin? If you understand the temporal aspect, then you won't take so much pride in the body that is now existing.

[*Maharaj is now talking about himself*] The body is thoroughly old, my mission is fulfilled. Now you people come, which is all right, but my mission is done. My soul is about to leave this body. I am happy. I clap! [*clapping his hands*] I am in a clapping mood that I am about to pass on. I am no longer in love with, or held by, anybody, anything, any attachment.

Forgetfulness—that noble, most elevated forgetfulness—will not arrive until all doubts have been dispelled. Unless the doubts are eradicated, that peace will not prevail.

So long as I remain identified with the body, I want to be occupied with actions, because I am not able to sustain that pure "I" without them. I cannot endure it, because I identify with the body-mind, with all kinds of activities. I call it *jiva-atman*, which means "conditioned by the body-mind," and is the self that is occupied with all the activities. And the "I" which is unconditioned by, and not identified with, the body-mind—that therefore has no form, design, or name—is *paramatman*. The *jiva-atman* is being witnessed by *paramatman*, which is your real Self only.

V: What is it doing? Is it partaking in the working of the world?

M: *Paramatman* need not participate in the activities of the world, but without that principle no activities could take place at all. Just as is the case with *akash* (space): without it, no activities are possible.

Activities are going on naturally, spontaneously, in the same way that there is no author or doer of your dream world. Nevertheless, you fully put to use your dream world. You will not be able to comprehend this so long as you try to understand things as an individual. But once you are the universal manifest consciousness and abide in that *paramatman* spirit—"I am" without form and distinction—then you will realize how things are.

V: It can be doubted whether Krishna was the incarnation of God into a human being. If it is indeed so, however, then we must attach importance to what he told us.

M: Whatever Krishna stated is perfectly correct. For that moment, that particular time in history, it was most appropriate. But that moment, that time, has gone. He also has gone. The spiritual elevation happened in him; that is why he is great.

You are seeing and understanding things through the concepts which you have absorbed. But, as a matter of fact, the actual state of affairs is quite different. You are holding on to it as the truth, but whatever you have heard will not remain as authority or as permanent; it will disappear. Then after the disappearance of everything, whatever remains, that you are: *neti-neti*.

You have been continuously changing; you are in a state of flux. No identity of yours has remained as a permanent feature. And in due course you will also become very old. So is there any constancy in all this?

V: The truth is that the body is perishable, but *Atma* is imperishable, eternal.

SECOND VISITOR: Do you know that or have you read it?

V: I am experiencing and also have read it. I am getting old and have seen people perish.

M: Yet there must be some author authorizing all these activities. You take the grosser four elements, which are engaged in activity. These four elements are presided over by space. In what activity is that engaged? If you are going to investigate the world of your observation, you will never reach your destination. Unless you give up whatever you have heard and abide in yourSelf, you will not understand all this. You may take it upon yourself to investigate this entire manifest world and whatever you have heard, but you will be caught more and more in a quagmire.

When incarnation takes place, what is its cause? And in what form does it occur? The stories you have heard...

V: Why doesn't everybody become Krishna?

M: What is that childhood? What is that child-principle? Investigate that. The touch of that quality, the child quality: understand and realize it. When did you encounter your-self? Since when and how? After collecting all the messages and concepts in the world, you cannot investigate yourself. When Krishna was born, he had that touch of "I-am-ness." The same goes for yourself. Understand that! What is that touch of "I-am-ness," that touch of child, in you? Since

when did you know that you are? And with what did you
know that you are? If you try to employ whatever you have
heard, you will never be able to understand this. You know
that you were not, but now you know that you are. How did
this happen, this confluence? You were not and suddenly
you are. This is what we want to discover.

V: I think I will give up on all this.

M: You just find out and enquire about your own self. Since
when did you come to know your self? And how? Did anybody tell you that you are? Or did you come to know yourself spontaneously?

V: I was told and also it kept occurring to me when I read
Ramana Maharshi's questions, "Who is it that dreams, who
is it that sleeps?"

M: Give up your body identity. Since when did you start
knowing yourself? Concentrate on that only.

V: Who is the one who slept?

M: Give up that question, because it is not relevant. There
is no value in your question. At the moment I do not want
you to ask any questions. I am driving you to the source
and would be satisfied with your knowing what you are. I
want to find out from you with what it is you know you are.
Confine yourself to this area. Focus only on your knowing
that "you are." How do you know you are? Just be there.
You have been shadow-boxing with the many concepts you
have collected from the world—you are fighting with all
that. What is the use of it?

You know you are. How do you know it? And with what
did you know it? This is the sum total of my teaching needed to put you on the right track, its very quintessence.

When all your questions are answered, my talks are very easy to understand. And when you understand, all your questions have gone. It is a vicious circle: So long as you have questions, you cannot follow what is being said.

V: What happens is that certain questions keep cropping up.

M: I am going for the basic questions only: What are you? Since when are you? How did you happen to be? And due to what are you? I don't want to deal with a lot of sundry questions; they are of no value to me. If you like my teachings, you may sit here; otherwise, by all means quit this place.

In any true spiritual search, whatever you have heard, whatever you have done, is of no use at all to arrive at the real truth. The knowledge "you are" has happened. Due to what?

First of all, you witness that you are. Stay put there only, with this "you are." Just be there. Then with the help of this "you are," you are witnessing the world. If you are not witnessing "you are," you will not be witnessing the world either.

When you do not know you are, people also will not know that you are and they will cremate you. So long as you know you are, people will respect you, as you are something. When you do not know you are, people will dispose of you. Stay put there. You must be present there only, at this point—the "you are" point, bereft of all concepts, all hearsay. When you recognize and realize the knowledge that you are, you will also know what Krishna is. Any number of incarnations have come and gone. But when you understand yourself, you will realize all the incarnations.

Because you know you are, you know the world is. You also know that God is. If you don't know you are, where is the world and where is the God?

There have been so many incarnations, and now you know you are. That "you are" is the divine principle because of which all the incarnations were. Many people have come here, but rarely has anybody, after listening to me, come closer to himself; rarely anyone will understand what I am driving at. But that rare person, in the process of understanding me, will come closer to himself, the one who listens. Those who really understand will abide in themselves.

You did not know your parents before your birth, nor did the parents know you. In spite of this, how did the knowledge "you are" sprout in that particular situation? What is this amazing thing? I am again putting the same question. The parents did not know the child, and the child also did not know his parents before his birth. Now the child says, Here I am. How is that?

This itself is the greatest miracle, that I got the news "I am." Have you any doubts that you are?

V: No, that is self-evident.

M: Prior to knowing that you are, what knowledge did you have? What question can you put here, at this point? What do you know?

Dhyana[3] means to have an objective. You want to consider something. You *are* that something. Just to be, you are. Just being the being, "I am." You meditate on something. That knowledge "I am" is yourself. Abide only there. How can you ask any questions at this point? Because that is the beginning of knowledge.

V: One should not ask any questions until one has achieved the goal. When one achieves that, the questions will be dissolved.

M: That is exactly what I am telling you. You know that "you are" is a very great miracle. This type of talk is not expounded anywhere else. The very source, the seed of this

---

3 *dhana*: meditation.

philosophy, nobody will expound. They will tell you to go and worship a certain God and you will get his blessing—you will be benefiting in such and such a way. Do this and you'll get that.

That deep urge to understand the truth is definitely going to occur. But if you desire to inquire into this entire objective[3] world and are captivated by it, you will never reach the goal.

By trying to learn all the history of Rama, Krishna, Christ, etc. you will not attain it either; you will never get satisfied. You will have that peace and quietude only when you know yourself, when you have that intimate knowledge "you are." You know you are. How did it happen to be with what you are? Because of what are you? What is the cause of it? Find out all that.

Your present capital is what you have read—whatever you have heard and read. But that type of investment is of no use in the spiritual field.

As I tell you, abide in yourself, be your own being, then only you will get that peace and quietude.

V: So I should not ask any questions?

M: Correct, no questions. Just be what you are. As I tell you, when you abide in your own self, all your questions will be dissolved by the knowledge "you are."

The manifested extends beyond any limits; it is spread all over, ample. If that knowledge "you are" is not there, where is the world? And where are the gods?

By reading various books and listening to everything else, you cannot become a *mahatma*, but only through that knowledge "I am." Don't concentrate on the body. Because of the body, you call yourself a male or a female. Just hold on to that knowledge "I am" only, with-

---

3 That is, the world of "objects," the external world.

out body sense—beyond name and form or design. But you have to employ name, form and design for the sake of worldly activities.

You are lucky, I am not expounding this in great detail to other people. To them, I simply say: You are "you," that knowledge "you are." Accept that only, and be on your way.

Don't meditate on anyone, any God or sage. And that knowledge "you are," don't embellish it with the body. I do not tell people more than they need and may not go into great detail. Because your parents have come to fruition, you are here at this moment. The knowledge that you are has no form and no name; it is purely knowledge "you are." A name and form is good only for the purposes of the world. Presently you are adjustable by the name; name means "myself." And to that name, you have given the disguise of the body. After relinquishing the name that is imposed on you, tell me your name. By hearing nobody, what can be your name?

V: No name!

M: Similarly, you accept the body as your identity. Right here and now, drop your identity with the body and sit still. Just drop this body like a discarded garment; drop also the identity with the name. And now you tell me about yourself. Whatever you are is most appropriate—that greatest principle that you are, about which you cannot give any information. But you are.

So long as you show that you are becoming more intimate with yourself, and getting to know that self, your comments are all right. The love for that knowledge "I am," the most lovable principle, is the knowledge "I am" itself. Is it not correct? That self, that knowledge "I am," has immense love for the self alone. But when that self or that love of the self becomes mixed up or associated with the body, the miseries begin.

V: One should have that realization of "I-ness," right?

M: Yes, but how can that happen unless you have full confirmation that "I am" is purely "I am"? You must have a firm conviction that "I am" is only that "I am," without body-mind form—the knowledge "I am" purely.

V: I am trying to do it, practice it.

M: When you say you are practicing that, it means you are developing your conviction. You are confirming your conviction about it. That is all. What other practice do you need?

V: What else is needed? Is there a technique for it?

M: That itself is the technique, because of which the world is. Male or female is the title of the body form, not of the *atman*, not of the Self.

V: I understand all this. It has been explained beautifully every day, we have read it in the books, we understand it, and that is why I have come here.

M: All these things are said by you, but has the knowledge come within the purview of the knowledge "I am"?

V: No.

M: You must have that full conviction, whatever you may have said. That is the truth and that is "I am." There are no techniques, except the technique that I am—the firm conviction that "I am" means "I am" only, abidance in "I."

V: I am trying to do that, and I think everyone here present is trying to do the same.

M: When a guru is really a *jnani*—that is, one who has realized himself—you should abide in him. When such a guru guides or directs a disciple, no spiritual technique is necessary. There was a time when Arjuna also was not doing any spiritual practice. All the armies were in the battle area, and the horses were ready to rush at the enemy. What time was available for Arjuna to practice? He just listened and accepted whatever Krishna told him, and that was all he needed to get realization. Arjuna reached the goal through his right attitude and because his guru, Krishna, was realized.

Don't practice this thing, only develop your conviction.

How long do you do this type of meditation? Until you stabilize in the conviction: I am the knowledge "I am." At that stage your individuality is completely extinguished; you no longer have a personality. And "you" denotes the manifested. In place of the lost individuality has come the manifest totality.

For a realized sage, there is no question of going into *samadhi* and descending from *samadhi*. So long as the so-called sage does not abide in that stage, in that Selfhood, until then he has to practice going into *samadhi* and coming down from *samadhi*.

V: By sage, you mean the individual?

M: A seeker. Normally the word *sadhaka* is used here, and also *mumukshi*. *Mumukshi* is a lower stage and means "inclined to spirituality." *Sadhaka* means one who thinks he is not "body-mind" but the manifest only.

6/7 July 1980

6.

Whatever You Can Forget Cannot be the Eternal

*V*isitor: Is it possible to tell me what to do step by step to come closer to realization?

Maharaj: Why does one have to do any practice and for what purpose?

V: Is no practice to be done then?

M: You remain confused so long as you are identified with your body. Even your question what is to be done is only from the point of view of your association with the body. As an individual, concerned with the body, what am I to do?— that really is your question. So long as you remain identified with the body, your confusion will continue.

V: Yes, intellectually it is clear. But when a realized person says that everybody is realized already, it would mean I am realized but I don't feel like it.

M: The person who says "I don't feel like it" is again identified with the body.

V: So I am unable to express whatever I feel.

M: Is it not something which is there and which you use? Without this consciousness you would not be able to think or do anything. So that which you are using is already there.

There is no other practice to be done, except to understand (that is, telling yourself with conviction) that it is this knowledge that you *are* which is itself the knowledge, and not the way you are using this knowledge at the individual level. So the knowledge itself is the one that exists and must remain pure in and as that knowledge; and you must remain apart from it. That knowledge that you *are* has mistakenly identified itself with the body and so you are thinking of yourself as the body. But you are the "knowledge." Strengthen your conviction that you are the knowledge, this beingness, and not the body.

V: How can one do so?

M: By meditation, like *dhyana*. And *dhyana* means the knowledge must remain in meditation with the knowledge. Now, what is meditation? Meditation is the knowledge "I am" remaining in that knowledge.

There is the waking state and the sleep state, and the knowledge that you are. I exist, I know that I exist. Other than that, what capital does anyone have than merely this knowledge "I am"?

V: I see it as being important because everything else is changing.

M: What can you base your questions on? The only thing that you have is the knowledge that you exist. Other than that, what knowledge do you have?

V: No knowledge, no other knowledge.

M: Therefore, be in that. And don't presume that you are someone to act. That is all you can do at this stage, and remain in that. All questions really come via your mind and the body, from which you have to be separate. This is the total message; remain in that. If you can accept this message, you may come here because you will repeatedly hear the same thing. But if it is not acceptable to you, then don't waste your time.

In the spiritual line, what work have you done? Have you read anything, done anything? Been anywhere?

V: Yes, in 1960 I became interested. At that time, I met Swami Menon [*presumably, the visitor is referring to Sri Krishna Menon, also known as Sri Atmananda*] and went to his lectures. I go to Ramanashram frequently, because there Maharaj's book was given to me by Sri Ganesan.

M: You read Ramana Maharshi? And both volumes of *I Am That*?

V: All the time. Ramana Maharshi's books and Maharaj's.

M: What has been said in Ramana Maharshi's books and what has been said in Maharaj's books—does it tally?

V: Absolutely. Ramana Maharshi is somewhat distant and gets you a little scared. Maharaj is tweaking your nose and talking, and easier to absorb.

M: You have a clear picture then of your true nature, of what you are?

V: In words, yes.

M: Even if you accept it in words, that is already a lot. Who is it that accepts what has been said in the words? Now that which accepts what has been said in the words, is that principle not separate from the words?

V: I am still a person with a memory. I hope to progress beyond that.

M: What makes you consider yourself as a person? Your identification with the body. Will this individual personality last? It will remain only so long as the identification with the body remains. But once there is a firm conviction that you are not the body, then that individuality is lost. It is the simplest thing, as soon as you have this conviction that you are not the body, then automatically, instantaneously, you become the total manifest. As soon as you leave your individuality, you become the manifest totality. But your true being is apart from even that which is totally manifest. And you assume this individuality within that total manifest so long as you are identified with the body.

When there is no individuality, what will you consider to be the one who meditates and the meditation? When this individuality is not there, who meditates and on what? People talk very freely of "meditation," but what do they really do? They use their consciousness to concentrate on something. *Dhyana* is when this knowledge, this consciousness that I am, meditates on itself and not on something other than itself.

V: On itself...

M: Knowledge has no form in any case.

V: So that is when the "I am" turns in on itself, it again gets qualified with form because that is the way I am to myself now.

M: When you say you must sit for meditation, the first thing to be done is understand that it is not this body identification that is sitting for meditation, but this knowledge "I am," this consciousness, which is sitting in meditation and is meditating on itself. When this is firmly understood, then it becomes easy. When this consciousness, this conscious presence, merges in itself, the state of *samadhi* ensues. When this *mana, buddhi, chitta,* or whatever names are being used, merges in that state, then even the knowledge "I am meditating" gets lost; this also becomes merged in that state. It is the conceptual feeling that I exist that disappears and merges into the beingness itself. So this conscious presence also gets merged into that knowledge, that beingness—that is *samadhi.*

That knowledge unfolds itself and begins to have the knowledge of everything movable and immovable. And that knowledge begins to know itself. And ultimately what happens? The conscious presence alone remains. That is, there is just conscious presence, not "I" or "you," or anything. I repeat: it is total presence; that is, total manifestation—not I, you or any individual.

This consciousness, which is within the body and therefore has mistakenly assumed that it *is* the body, gradually realizes its true nature, namely that it is only conscious presence without any inherent individual aspects. Finally, it considers itself the conscious presence of the total manifestation, and all individuality is lost.

Thus, what starts as selfishness (in the individual sense, as identification with the individual) ultimately becomes knowledge of the Self, as conscious presence.

Have you any comment on this? When you ask questions, ask them on the basis that you are not the body-mind, but that you are the conscious presence.

V: It seems that Maharaj is describing two aspects of meditation on the beyond. First is this concentration—consciousness turning in on itself, the sense "I am"— and then, from that standpoint and only then can the conscious being observe with what it has identified itself and free itself from all these identifications.

The only thing that I come up against occasionally is that during the course of meditation some very powerful forces get released in the body and try to shake it sometimes, and at other times there are visions or psychic experiences. All one has to do during such times, what I understand from Maharaj, is to hold to the sense "I am" and try to observe what is happening even though it can tend to distract one very strongly from this sense of presence.

M: That is true, except understand that you are not actually doing the witnessing. Of whatever happens, sitting in the morning, or the visions that come to you, merely look at them, but understand that *you* are not looking at them, there is no "you" as an entity witnessing them; witnessing takes place by itself. So just be in your meditation, and witnessing takes place of whatever there is to be witnessed. And don't even involve yourself in the witnessing. There is daylight outside. Well, we see it; we don't have to make a statement: Ah, I am seeing the daylight there! So, *we* are not witnessing; witnessing takes place automatically.

V: One of the interesting things happening in America in the last few years has been the tremendous importance attached to giving people body massages and things like that to kind of artificially free up the flow of this life force through the body. I feel this is a purely mechanical thing, and sooner or later all the old stuff comes back again. But if we open ourselves in the way that Maharaj instructs us, you can just naturally feel all these little areas of contraction in the body melting away. And it seems to me this is one minor but still important reason for the spiritual aspect which he is presenting to us.

INTERPRETER: He presently does not have enough strength to talk about that. When people refer to devotion, they devote themselves to God, but it is actually devotion to the vital force. All these yogis, what they are doing is they are devoting their time to the vital force.

V: Does he mean by that the play of the vital force through the whole *chakra* system, and that they do all these exercises to manipulate the spine to elicit various effects?

M: The most important thing is the vital force. Whatever names are given for doing all the spiritual practices, ultimately these efforts apply to the vital force only, because without that there is no existence at all, there is no consciousness. So the vital force is the most important. Whenever the vital force is there, that "I"-consciousness, the knowledge "I am," is there.

And then there are the four kinds of speech. *Para* and *pashyanti* refer to existence; and all the activities happen through *madhyama* and *vaikhari*. *Madhyama* means the mind, and *vaikhari* is the speech as expressed, the words that ultimately come out through the mouth.

People are directed to other things, but nobody tells them about this birth principle, *sattva*. That birth principle contains everything; all these four kinds of speech and everything else are contained in it. Not only that, the whole universe, everything that appears, is contained in the birth principle. This is the reason so much stress is placed on finding out what it is. Few people give attention to that birth principle, because they don't realize its importance. Because of the birth principle, everything is, the world is. All the knowledge of the world is contained in it. Only one in a crore (ten million) persons can find out what the birth principle is. And once you know it, everything, all knowledge, belongs to you—even liberation is yours.

Then there is that nine-month period in the womb. So what is the content of the womb? It is that knowledge "I am" in dormant condition. That is being developed slowly. So within that birth principle, everything is contained.

INTERPRETER: To people who criticize a lot but don't know anything, or somebody who claims to know too much, Maharaj jokingly says, You have not come out of the womb too fast. So everything, all knowledge, is contained in that womb, he says.

He has found certain changes taking place in his body—something extraordinary. For example, when you examine his pulse, some kind of inner strength is sensed. How do all these things happen? He says that the disease is for the birth principle, whereas, he being the witness of the birth principle, is unaffected. Because he has no birth, there is also no possibility of death. So he just witnesses all these things. He has passed all that on to the birth principle, he says, being the knower of it. Thus, the disease applies to the birth principle only. It has appeared and ultimately what the disease can do, is to extinguish that birth principle. But I am not that, he says; therefore, he is unconcerned with it.

Recognize what he is. In order to recognize him, you have to follow his method. He told you that your consciousness is God. Now once you understand that you are not the body but the consciousness, then you get stabilized or established in God's womb. When you go there, you can know what he is. Until then, you don't. That is why he says, so many people have come and gone but nobody has recognized him correctly. They come here and have frequent meetings, and then they say that they follow him. Ultimately, they will come to know that they are the *Brahman*. But still they don't know me, he says. The knower of *Brahman*, they don't know.

You are still within the realm of consciousness; you are to transcend consciousness to know him.

The effect of the disease will be that the memory of the birth will disappear. I am not affected, he says. So long as that remnant ink is available, there is a recording done; that applies to the causal body also. When the ink gets dried up, that causal body is also out of questions.

He says, some people have come to him who have realized. No doubt about it. They are *jnanis*, but not *Brahmajnanis*. They have stabilized in the consciousness. They have understood the godhead, that they are God, but could not transcend it. *Brih* means "world" and *aham* means "I," "I am." So world together with "I am" ("I am the world")—that is *Brahman*.

For forty-two years he has talked so much that he does not like to talk much now. Although people listen to him, they don't get rid of their concepts; therefore, they remain ensnared within their concepts. In order to really understand what he says, you have to worship that *prana*, the vital force. That meditation is necessary.

M: Wherever there is some sound, there must be something responsible for it. Now the world is there, so something must have been responsible for its appearance. So that is consciousness. Consciousness is there, therefore the world is. Now, in whose presence, can you say, is the eternal truth, the absolute principle? *Turiya* means where the consciousness is. One who knows *turiya* is *turiyatita*. That is my state. *Turiya* is within the consciousness, which is the product of the five elements. And one who transcends that, who knows the *turiya*, is *turiyatita*. In order to be stabilized in *turiya*, you must know the birth principle.

V: *Turiya* is always described as the witness state that sees through waking, dreaming and sleeping. And *turiyatita* is beyond even that.

M: That which is called birth, the birth principle itself, is *turiya*. The experience that you exist itself is *turiya*.

At this moment, whatever you are, its principle has a

beginning. It had to originate somewhere. It may be any God, Krishna, Rama, or anybody. But it had to originate at some point. Without birth principle, what is there?

I: There is no reservation, you know. He does not spare anyone, he just talks straight.

V: Tell him I saw that very vividly yesterday with a friend whom I brought here.

I: He says he can talk like that because he has no doubts whatever about what is and what is not. That is why his talk is of this kind. There is no "perhaps," or "suppose," and all that kind of thing.

V: It must be very frustrating for him when people come here and just cling blindly and adamantly to some concept and think they can find a solution through a little manipulation of that.

M: Many sages in the past have proved their victory over mind. For example, there was Mirabai—Mirabai was a great saint—and she was given poison by her husband. But nothing happened to her.

Then there is the story of another sage. This one was sick and had not taken medicine for a very long time, and all his disciples were very worried. So they said to him, you must take medicine. He answered, bring all your medicines, and he gulped down the whole thing. And they were again worried. But again nothing happened. Now this also is victory over mind.

Victory over mind is one thing; a better expression would be stabilizing in the Self: conviction about your true nature.

One common characteristic of these sages is that they know what they are. They identify themselves with the supreme Self. So if somebody tells them about birth, death, sickness, they don't accept all that; they don't believe it, because they have no doubts about what they really are.

V: You might put me out of business! I will go home and tell any patients who come to see me it is all in their head.

M: Of all the statements that I have heard, I have not accepted any except my guru's, that I am *Brahman*. That is the only acceptable statement to me.

A man came here from Baroda and gave me some number and said, you will become a millionaire, overnight. I said, don't give me that, you give it to other people who are here. Because tomorrow, in the same manner, you will tell me I am going to die. So if I am going to become a millionaire, I can die also. It is of no value to me. So many people have come, including many doctors. They have said so much; I have just looked at them and ignored whatever they told me.

We, as concepts, accept them and make them our own; it has become very difficult to reject them. I am not the product of my parents. They have not created me. I have come about spontaneously. In your case, you just think whether your parents attached those eyes here, put the nose there, and the mouth...Whatever information I have prior to birth, that is the only correct information. That knowledge is *Parabrahman*. Prior to birth is the Absolute, *Parabrahman*. And after birth is *chetana-parabrahman*, the manifest *Brahman* or the consciousness *Brahman*.

I am that principle which was not affected when the universe was dissolved so many times.

This "I am" concept was not there prior to what you call "birth." So as this concept has appeared, it will also go away. How am I affected? In no way whatsoever. Because it is not true. This applies to all concepts. Prior to birth, and after birth, whatever knowledge I have, my own, without hearing it from anyone, that is the only true knowledge which I accept. And the proof lies in my guru's words.

I tell people whatever is correct. I need not read the Vedas to learn from them, but prior to what is called my birth, whatever knowledge I already had, I am getting confirmation of it in the Vedas.

In this world, it is common practice for human beings to ask others for knowledge in both worldly and spiritual matters. And from that they try to live—knowledge gathered from others, not their own. People learn whatever they are taught. What they were, prior to being taught, nobody gives attention to. Whatever you can forget, cannot be the eternal; it cannot be the truth. That is why you cannot forget your true state, and that is why you cannot remember it. Whatever you forget, is not the truth, always remember that.

People come here to ask questions, but what do they know in order to ask questions? Do they have any knowledge of themselves? Do they have any real knowledge? Whatever they have read, heard, or have been taught they regurgitate.

We identify ourselves with the name given us. And what is that name? It is whatever occurred to our parents. We are so much attached to that name; we act with it constantly in the world. And this name is an accident; the word that occurred to their minds is my name, and in this accidental thing I am taking my form.

This lady here usually tells her husband what she has heard at these talks. But today this is going to be very difficult for her. Because this knowledge is beyond words. How can you put this into words?

Normally the thought flow is continuous, always there. How much of that thought flow is useful to you? Of all these thoughts, take only those that are useful to you. Sometimes, I command thoughts to get out: "I don't want to have anything to do with you." Fewer than one in a thousand people will ever wonder what is the use of all these thoughts that are just flowing.

V: Very few stop to think about thinking.

M: When thought has no customers, thought vanishes; there is no thought.

V: Yet, when he is teaching us, the thoughts are so clear and well defined. It is a paradox.

M: I have no faith in any religion, including Hinduism.

When you first come here, just listen to what is going on, try to understand it. Even if questions arise, don't ask them for the time being—just listen. For now I will be talking about that power which looks like an individual but because of whose presence the world is carrying on its business. It may not be easily comprehensible, but I can't be bothered to go into much detail and explain everything at this stage. So try to understand as much as you can; otherwise, let it go.

I am talking about this power which is in the body, but which is the root of the existence and maintenance of the entire universe. What there is in my body, is in everyone else's body also. But everyone else is concerned more about this "corpse" that he is living with rather than that which lies within that corpse. Whatever upheavals occur in the world, they are movements in that power, for it is that which makes the world go around. And whatever events take place are movements in that consciousness. Because we associate ourselves with the events, there is unhappiness. I see things from a different standpoint, from the point of view of the Absolute.

So what is your query?

V: Well, it is just the impersonality of this power, and how nobody seems to have any capacity to control or manipulate it. Most us in the West think we can though, which is the biggest part of the illusion. And sometimes, things seem to go one's way, but at other times they seem to go very much against what you believe to be right and proper.

M: Whatever is happening is bound to happen. There is a series of events; a scenario is written down. So according to that scenario, things happen. If we are identified with all sorts of things, we have certain hopes and aspirations; and if things turn out accordingly, we are happy. If the things that happen are not according to our wishes, we are unhappy. So we will continue to be happy and unhappy in an endless cycle, so long as we persist in this attitude. However, the moment we see things in proper perspective—that all we can do is to see that witnessing happens, and that whatever happens is independent of our thoughts—then there is a different state. There is no volition as far as an individual is concerned; things happen on their own. When that is seen, there is already a certain peace of mind.

Whatever people complain about, the five elements are not bothered. So why should what happens in the five elements bother the individual? If the five elements themselves are not bothered by what people think and what they do or not do, how is this source of those elements, upon which they depend, concerned? Why would it be concerned?

Some time ago, I had suggested to you to read the Gita from the standpoint of Lord Krishna, not from that of Arjuna. Now even when doing that, you must understand what I meant by Lord Krishna. I did not mean Lord Krishna as an individual personality. I meant by Lord Krishna that speck of consciousness within you that I am, that "I-am-ness." That is Lord Krishna, this "I-am-ness," and you should read the book from that viewpoint. As far as anybody is concerned, could there be the world, could there be God, could there be anything at all in the absence of that Krishna consciousness?

V: No, I don't believe so.

M: The moment this is clearly understood, that is it. There is nothing further to be done. And whatever people continue to do or think they are doing, they are purely a concept based on a certain image they have of themselves. And once they act according to that image, they will be susceptible to all kinds of unhappiness. Whatever happens is a mere movement in that consciousness. Once this is understood, nothing remains to be done: there is nothing you can or need to do.

V: There remains a kind of paradox in the sense that when one embarks on a consideration of the spiritual life, certain decisions have to be made to minimize, or at least economize, one's worldly activities so that one may have more time available for such consideration. There is also some sense of urgency involved in this, probably still because of the illusion of being this person. But if in the enlightened state there is simply this posture of passive witnessing, how is it that these decisions get made and how is it that they are carried through?

M: Only this concept that you have about yourself, that is what decides. Whether he be a big man, an important man, or a small man, whatever he decides, or thinks he decides, it is purely a concept. That is, the individual as an object thinks he can decide, but in fact no object can decide. If he does not understand, then the whole thing is conceptual. It is to be understood that the body-mind complex is merely an object, a phenomenon; and no phenomenon can act. So the concept is very much involved in your body-mind complex.

You will never be able to grasp your true nature; for this, the center of perception must change. If that center of perception is a phenomenon, then whichever way you look, that looking is still from the center of the phenomenon. So unless that center of perceiving itself is changed to the Noumenon, you will never get an idea of your true nature.

Who has decided that I am the body? Purely a concept. This concept is, of course, on the level of the mind. So it is only a concept that I am the body. And it is equally a concept that whatever action takes place, it is done by this body; that is, there has been an "objectivization," a concept that I am this object, the body. From then on, it is the concept that whatever the body does, is my doing. But once this concept is understood—that is, once the object is known as an object, the false as the false—then you take the standpoint of the subject.[1] Once you take that standpoint, the object disappears. And you view whatever takes place as a happening in the condition, and you are not concerned with it; you are merely viewing it.

That I am the body and an individual personality means I am time-bound. There is a measure of time. That same concept which has taken to saying I am the body, will say, I am born and will die. Who says, I will die? Only the concept. Once you are away from the concept, the subject has no time in it. There is no space-time concept as far as the subject is concerned.

I repeat, not only is it this concept that says "I am the body," but it is also conscious of the fact that it is time-bound; thus, it says, I will die. But the one who knows the concept is not time-bound; he is quite apart from the concept. The body dies. This means what? It means only the thought "I am," that concept, has disappeared. Nothing has happened to the knower of the whole happening.

One who knows that this is a concept and that the concept will disappear, does not have the experience of either the birth, the happiness or unhappiness, or the death.

---

1 Not to be understood in the usual sense of a "doer" or a person-like "entity," since the term as used by Maharaj has no particular focus or location in space–time. In this connection, the term "subjectivity," without these familiar associations, has been used alternatively.

V: Maharaj was saying that we are all subject to this power, and we can do nothing over and against this power; it is really just a concept in our mind, and it never works out. Well, in a sense, from the standpoint that we come to him, the arising of enlightenment in an individual would seem to be quite apart from any volitional activity.

M: The whole object of the spiritual search or quest—there is no quest really, but we just use that word here for the sake of communication—is to understand the concept as a concept, the false as the false. There is nothing to be acquired.

That I am God or that I am Christ, Allah, Muhammad, or whatever it is, is still based on the concept "I am." Because, unless that concept is reneged, all that you build on it will still be an illusion. So ultimately, only when this "I-am-ness" itself disappears, will you be free of the concept. So long as the basic concept "I am" is there, the conceptual element cannot disappear. It is the concept itself that has given various names to itself, but it is still the same concept.

Without this basic concept "I am," where is the world, God, where is Ishwara, Christ, Allah, anyone? Before this concept of "I am" came on you, were you happy or unhappy? Was there even any feeling of happiness or unhappiness? Any of the dualities?

V: I don't know.

M: I had no experience of happiness or unhappiness because this concept "I am" was not there.

V: Nor was there any awareness of that fact.

M: Whatever conceivable thing or feeling, or thought, it can come only when there is this basic "I-am-ness." The basic "I-am-ness" itself was not there. So, *who* was to know, *who* was to be aware? The very feeling of existence was not there. That I am, that I exist, the feeling, the concept itself was not there, so who was to have any feeling? Who was to have any awareness, who was to have any consciousness?

If I am a yogi, a king, or whatever, this consciousness that I am, this "I-am-ness," imagination, mind, call it what you like, is only this concept. Before this concept arose, was there anything? There was nothing. There was not even any happiness or unhappiness: the perfect state.

V: I think the other thing that was absent and gives rise to so may of our questions is the sense of time. For example, why was I not aware in the past? If there is some understanding, there is no past.

M: Exactly. When one talks of consciousness, one is likely to think in terms of an individual. But understand that it is not really the individual that has consciousness, but it is the consciousness that assumes innumerable forms.

I keep repeating that the average person will not understand this. Why? Because it is too simple! To grasp, one wants something, some form, some shape. That "something" is born, and is going to die or disappear is all imagination, all an illusion—nothing is born. It is the child born of a barren woman. Who calls it that? Even that is a concept. Because in the absence of the basic concept "I am," there is no thought, no awareness, no consciousness of one's existence.

[*To one of the visitors in particular*] What about that actor friend of yours? Will he reach the state of absorbing what has been said now?

V: [*To the interpreter*] Tell him, he is at home licking his wounds. Another feeling or idea I just wanted to put to Maharaj, while on the subject of concepts, especially this fundamental concept "I am," is that we tend to confuse it with all the crude, ill-formed thoughts that...but in a sense *this* concept is like the most subtle activity right at the very touchstone of consciousness; you can miss its fundamental nature if you just consider it in the way that we ordinarily use the word "concept."

M: One in ten million will grasp the subtle part of the whole thing.

V: The total population of Bombay! But obviously the Maharaj has not got disheartened either. He has been talking for forty-two years. How many times has he seen anybody for whom he has held out any hope at all?

M: Even then, it is a concept again. But I give you a criterion by which one can sort of judge something.

When a stage is reached that one feels deeply that whatever is being done is happening and one has not got anything to do with it, then it becomes such a deep conviction that whatever is happening is not happening really. And that whatever seems to be happening is also an illusion. That may be final. In other words, totally apart from whatever seems to be happening, when one stops thinking that one is living, and gets the feeling that one is being lived, that whatever one is doing, one is not doing, but *one is made to do*, then that is sort of a criterion.

V: The teacher in the West who has his disciples ask themselves that question, who is the one who is living you now...

M: It can never be announced.

V: That is true.

M: If an answer is given, it can only be at the mind level. If there is someone who has done a lot of *sadhana*, and having done that, still has not achieved anything, he will have questions to ask, such as "What have I been doing wrong?"

V: One of the obvious answers for a lot of people who come here is that they have been waiting for Maharaj's teaching to come into their lives.

M: How do all people in the world, successful or otherwise, operate? When you look into it, you will find that everyone has assumed a "sample," a certain image of himself. I am so and so—an image or a pose. And it is from that pose that he is acting. That pose has been taken by his concept about himself. And only someone who understands this—the source of his actions—becomes free of it. He sees the false as the false.

These godmen, even *rishis*, *munis*, who consider themselves avatars, every single one of them, are doing the same thing. They have assumed a certain pose, based on a particular concept. And unless they also see why they are acting and how they are acting from that pose, based on concept, they will continue to do so and not be free from it.

V: I have often felt that everybody in this world is trying to present some sort of face, and all our activities are in aid of maintaining that sense of the self we have, to protect us from having to look beyond it.

We were making some funny remarks about psychiatrists yesterday. Until they begin to understand that so many of people's neurotic behaviors occur when this face they are trying to present is being threatened or challenged in some way, I don't think they will ever know what they are doing.

M: Psychiatrists will have first to understand what mind *is*, not how the mind works, but what mind itself is. Then there may be some change.

V: It is a long way off.

M: It is indeed.

V: Because they are never going to learn that from books. That is where everybody thinks he is going to learn it from.

M: The Marathi word for psychiatrist is *mana-shastri*; that is, *mana* is mind, so "doctor of the mind." Unless the doctor of the mind first understands what mind is, he will not get anywhere. Whatever goes on is based on the mind. The main question he should address in the first place is: What is it that the mind itself is based on? What is that of which mind is the content? Then he will get somewhere. Whatever goes on in the world is based on concept. The concept in action is "mind." Have you thoroughly understood the fact that you are not the concept but the knower of the concept? Whatever names and designations exist in the world, they are all of concept. And you are not the concept. What I say, has it now acquired some familiarity?

V: Very much so. I have tried to live with it for the past two years, every day of my life.

M: It is not something to be put into practice easily. Only look at yourself. This is "you." There is nothing to be done! I will never let you get away from it. Nothing to be lived; in fact, that is what was said earlier. When you realize what is living, what you think you are living, is that you are merely being lived. Whatever you may think you have understood, whatever is your knowledge, it is all a concept. *Rishi*, *muni*, yogi, king, whoever he may be, is all based on concept, a pose taken.

V: One thing that has baffled me for some time is with respect to a man I came across, with all sorts of miraculous powers who very obviously professed himself as such and such, an avatar. This seems to me a concept which is not true to the essence of what India has always stood for and

Maharaj so obviously represents. With my scientific background, I could not doubt the veracity of this man's claims, once I was able to observe what happened to people before and after the performance of a particular miracle. But I have found it hard to understand why a man with such incredible control over the workings of nature and his ability to manipulate it, did not seem to have the same degree of insight back into what are the seeds of this whole concept.

M: Is this someone in San Francisco?

V: No, no, I am talking of Sai Baba.

I: He always goes to the root of any matter. He says, there is Sai Baba. So what is Sai Baba? When we say Sai Baba, what is Baba, and how is it Baba? And earlier he said, why open someone else's shop?

V: It does not matter to me.

I: When he had the energy, he used to speak a lot. Whoever came at any level, he would speak to him. But now that he is not too well, he says he wants to speak only to some scientists with specialized knowledge of the subject, of the five elements. So he would be able to challenge whatever is being said. Otherwise, he says, it would be a waste of energy, of which he is already depleted.

V: After a while that (scientific) knowledge—and that is what I am engaged in—is very boring. It is ever the same, and it does not fulfill you.

July 7/8, 1980

7.

YOU ARE THAT WHICH OBSERVES THE COMING AND GOING OF THE CONSCIOUSNESS

*V*ISITOR: One of the things that Maharaj was talking about this morning is how the life force in our bodies, the *prana*, would not have been able to appear without consciousness being present.

MAHARAJ: When you understand that this knowledge-consciousness is your very thought, and as your conviction about that increases, you become desireless. Then, gradually you let go of all desires; they drop away.

With medicine, can one make a condition endurable?

V: Each case has to be taken on its own merits. You can't make a universal law. Yes, in my experience this can happen. You can't say, yes, it definitely will happen. That is just not the way it works.

M: We must have death without pain. Most of the great sages in India died of cancer. We had one sage, some three centuries ago, by the name of Tukaram. He was doing *bhajans* and at the last moment he just disintegrated into nothingness. No pain, no body, nothing. All he left were probably his sandals and sitar, that string instrument. He just vanished. We have three or four other sages like that, who just disappeared into thin air. Mirabai was another one; she merged into an idol. In the South, there was a sage from Bengal. He went to Puri [city in Orissa State], and he also merged into an idol...no remnants. So I said that is the best type, and if they could pass on this skill to all of us, we would be immensely grateful.

V: The story I heard about Tukaram was not that he decided to die, but he was with his disciples, and he was so disgusted with their lack of response to his teaching that he said I am going to leave you. He entered this little room, with only one door and no windows at all, while the devotees were sitting outside. After some time, they went inside and found no trace of him.

INTERPRETER: Maharaj does not want people to hang on to him for long periods. They should receive the talks, understand, and abide in them even while being away from him.

M: Spirituality is very necessary to keep oneself alive. Having understood what is what, you come to the conclusion that death is also an illusion. A *jnani* is one who abides in the Absolute, who is the Absolute only. A *jnani* who has understood and transcended this consciousness does not want to prolong the life of consciousness. He leaves consciousness to its own nature, to spontaneity; he does not interfere.

Of a *jnani*, nobody can say he has any relatives: all could be his relatives or none could be. Only a *jnani* knows that everything is not, everything will not be, and everything has never been. For a *jnani*, individuality has been liquidated completely; there is only manifest consciousness, which is ample and plenty for him.

V: He is saying there is no identification with that.

M: A *jnani* has transcended consciousness, although the association with consciousness is still there. And consciousness, "I-am-ness," represents manifestation in its totality, because it is not confined or conditioned by the body as an "individual."

As are the concepts occurring to a person, so will be his behavior. This "I am" itself is the primary concept, and from that flow all others. According to you, what is your identity? With what identity do you exist in this world?

V: Well, I try to detach myself from any identity.

M: Yes, but who tries to detach from any identity? Who is it who detaches also from that identity? What is the nature of that particular identity or entity which wants to get rid of the suffering? Is it the happiness or is it something else? What do you think?

V: Maybe, the feeling of dissatisfaction.

M: You have a feeling that happiness is there, and you have a feeling that suffering is there. Between these two points, where are you? Who are you to find out this feeling of happiness and that feeling of suffering?

V: I found there is actually nobody there. There is only the suffering.

M: The fact that there is nobody, no entity to feel like that, are you really convinced of it?

V: Well, the conviction is based on practicing.

M: Nobody is there, nobody is existing there, that's what you are saying; there is no identity whatsoever; that "nobody," is it wearing this garb now? [*The questioner wears a monastic robe.*]

V: No, the difficulty is there is still some sense of attachment.

M: Since when do you know that you are?

V: Maybe since I was born.

M: Did you have any experience of your birth, or you just heard about it?

V: There are only vague memories of very early childhood, and images.

M: That is, you have heard about your birth, but you don't know anything yourself directly.

V: I must have heard about it also.

M: You know that you are, because you have heard that you were born. Therefore, you are. You say "I feel I am" since my birth, but you *only heard* of your birth.

V: And that is more or less interrelated with one's environment. The memories build up a sense of self-identity.

M: Regardless of what you have heard about being born, that particular identity is this, is it not? Whatever you feel you are, is it not the form? The same form, is it not, of which you have heard that it was born and signified *your* birth?

V: You mean I stay in the same identity with which I was born?

M: You have heard about the form being born. And this is the form. You call it now your identity, whatever you call yourself. You have heard you were born and you are experiencing that birth only now, isn't it? From the moment you are experiencing the world, you are experiencing the birth.

All that you understand is objective knowledge, which is impermanent and will not remain with you. The one who says, I don't understand, that is "you." You are that particular thing that says I don't know. And whatever you know, whatever is an objective perception, is all impermanent.

V: Doesn't that imply the sense of "me" as well?

M: If you say you have a sense of "me," that is not going to remain with you; it is impermanent. Once again, it is *anatma*. So why be bothered with that? Why worry about a thing that is not permanent? So where is your question now?

The one who says "I don't know," does he exist prior to the one who says I know? There is something which says I know and there is something in you which says I don't know. Which is prior?

V: There must be something existing before. What we mean by "I know," I don't know. I know if it is just knowledge based on objects that are impermanent.

M: That which knows it is impermanent is existing all the time. Without this knowledge, you cannot make the statement "I don't know." All objective knowledge is impermanent.

V: But then what is so-called "Self-realization"?

M: We will come to that a little later. Self-realization means I am completely full, I don't want to know anything [*laughter*], I don't require anything at all now. Self-realization is a term, a goal which we are trying to understand. If it is an outside answer, it cannot be reached. Unless it undulates within you, that means you are that, you will not be able to understand it. It cannot come from outside. Those are the only terms and goals, and no path leads to it. There is nothing more to be understood, since you are that. If you understand this, that is all. Then whatever objective understanding is impermanent, that entity which knows is permanent, which you will never be able to understand.

V: The thing is complete already, and I have failed to realize that. I am trying all these days to be one with that.

SECOND VISITOR: But as long as we try this, there is a sense of separation involved. That means in a way the trying must stop.

M: You cannot try that, you know. It must be there already. You say, it is perfect, is it not? Then where is the question of reaching the perfection? You cannot reach something which you are not. You must be perfect right from the beginning. Therefore, you are that. You don't have to reach something.

You are trying to create a goal. Only your mind is creating something, you see. You don't know the fact at all, because you *are* the fact. How are you going to know a fact as an objective thing? That is, if it is a fact, it is subjective. You cannot know it as other than you.[1] If you are going to know it as other than you, it becomes objective, it is impermanent.

That is why all people are after spiritual pursuits, you see. They go with one hand out, they want something to be blessed. But if somebody blesses you, you put out another hand and you say bless me here also. Self-realization is not to be given on a platter. It is already there. What is there to be given? That which can be given to you, has to be secured. You don't require any security, or anything at all. It is already there. If you feel it is not there, you are never going to realize it.

---

1 That is, dualistically, in a subject-object relationship.

V: Some instruction helps, though.

M: If you are getting the instructions according to a certain path or method, then again you will get into trouble. There is nothing like that; there is no path, no instruction at all. That you must understand.

V: There are strong habit patterns.

M: Yes, and once you know their impermanence and that they are not true, why worry about the habit patterns? Remove the habit. Go beyond! If you cannot do so, then you cannot understand this, the whole final truth, yet. No path, no instruction, no method, no technique. You are full, you are all One. You feel you are two, so OK. *Understand* you are not two, *advaita*.

You were a child, and you have become a big boy now, a big man. Do you know anything about along which path you have come? And how you have grown? You don't know anything about this? Then why do you want to ask which path to follow now?

I would like to know the path by which you have come into this life and have grown into this man. If you tell me, then I will tell you the path to go back.

These are all ideas, concepts! A grand idea that you were born and you are growing, and you have come this way, that way. There are people who told you this. So I want you to go back to the source from where you seem to have come. Stop there and find out. Look back, and see what is happening there. Don't go with the current and then see what is what. You will never be able to find out, because your travel in the stream is only conditioned...with concepts. You have heard about things from people, you have read about it in books. That is why you are passing along the stream, is it not? Go back. Go to its source and find out whether there is anything. That is the beauty of my teaching. It takes you back to the source and does not allow you to leave that source at all. If you want to discuss anything regarding what happened to you after entering the stream, OK, then so many stories abound. All the scriptures of Hindu as well as other religions, are available to you. Go and read them. They are of no use. But I say you can go back. Go back to that point from where you seem to have come, and see if you have really come. That will require meditation, and you will have to constantly return to that point. You will have to have full attention on it and find out really and truly whether you are actually coming from there, whether you are really born. Until then, they are all stories which you hear in listening to people.

V: A certain amount of awareness to be able to go back is required.

M: Awareness of what? You are already aware of so many things, are you not? You must be aware of the correct thing, mustn't you? You are already aware of everything: whatever is happening around you, you are aware of. You can't do anything without being aware. So your attention must be on this source, that is all.

V: Well, awareness must be there always.

M: But you are not aware of that awareness, which must be there.

V: One is not always focused on this to the same degree.

M: In the awareness also you are moving with the conditioning, because your consciousness is nothing but a bundle of concepts, ideas—whatever you have gathered right from childhood.

V: That means, the point of awareness is in the present moment only?

M: If you are really conscious of everything you see, would you ever try to enter the consciousness and thereby drag yourself down into the suffering? Consciousness brings you trouble, does it not? The very moment you became conscious that you are, the trouble started. Whatever suffering you are talking about began only when the consciousness came upon you.

Suppose somebody wants to *be*; being rooted in the consciousness means once again being rooted in the suffering and whatever comes out of that. All you need to understand is the nature of the consciousness and feel that you have nothing to do with it. Consciousness is a guest with you, is it not? It was not there, and in future it is not going to be there either; it remains with you temporarily. And in that temporary knowledge about the consciousness, you want to understand everything in that consciousness itself. What can you really understand in the consciousness? Unless and until you try to be aware of this consciousness, which is coming and going, which is conditioning—concepts, ideas, hopes, and all the things...

V: So the awareness must be beyond consciousness?

M: It is already beyond consciousness. If awareness is there, that is where the consciousness appears on.

Now the body is there for you. The body is made of what? Elements, is it not? If for once you understand that you are not the elements...You exist prior to the coming of the elements.

The moment the consciousness of "I" appears on you, you have the experience of the world. Therefore, you have the experience of suffering as well as happiness. Try to know the nature of this suffering and happiness, which is coming through the consciousness into the mind. And once you understand that, you know that you are not anything of the sort; then that's all. Suffering has nothing to do with you, happiness also has nothing to do with you. It is all happening in the consciousness, and you are observing the consciousness coming and going. All this is known by something in you; this is your nature, you are That. That cannot be understood as an objective thing. The moment the consciousness comes and the moment it goes away from you, you are understanding that everyday, is it not? Is it not in your experience?

In the sleep state you are not conscious, in the waking state you are conscious; that means all these things are there, you are there, you know that. Who knows that? Who knows the coming and going of the consciousness? The particular thing that knows it is "You," that is your true nature. Do you understand that?

V: Yes, I understand intellectually, but I still cannot grasp it.

M: But where is the question of grasping? And understanding it intellectually also? We always say, I have understood intellectually and I have grasped intellectually; but where is the question? It is a fact, is it not? Do you have to understand each and every fact by the intellect only? It is a fact, you know it now, that's all—it is that simple.

Since you have been doing *sadhana* for five and a half years, do you have any honest recognition of the identity in you which is permanent? You have the consciousness which knows the world, but you also know it comes and goes. Now, do you know what it is in you that remains always, which is not coming or going but is permanently there? Were you able to find that out within these five and half years of whatever you have been doing? You see there is a principle in you, which we call *chetana* or consciousness, which is the common factor, because in *chetana* you are moving, you are doing everything. But you also know this comes and goes. Consciousness is not permanent. When consciousness comes, you call it birth, when it goes you call it death. So that also is not a permanent identity. Have you any other knowledge about a permanent identity within you, which always remains with you, and never goes away?

V: I cannot really say that I have such knowledge.

M: You have accepted this fact right from the beginning when you say I don't know anything. So we are now pointing out the "you"; that which says "I don't know anything" is your real nature, you are That. And that which you know, is not real; it is impermanent.

That which you know, which you can perceive with your eyes, is not true. And that which says, I don't know anything, that is your true nature. You are That, and you cannot find it out as an objective thing. The moment it becomes objective, it is impermanent, so it is not true.

V: So actually, it cannot be explained then.

M: Naturally, it has already been stated everywhere that it cannot be explained, it cannot be described; it can only be pointed out. So whatever I am pointing to, look at that particular point, don't look at the finger which points out to you. You are only looking at the finger; you are not looking at the point which is showing. The finger is not the thing!

Any question?

V: How far can any questions be of use if we cannot explain?

M: Unless and until you are once again the image, you are not going to ask me a question. Otherwise, you are one with me.

There is no change in your state. You were perfect before you came here, and now that you are returning you are also perfect. There can't be any change anywhere at all. But you feel there is a change now, so you are happy. Go back with happiness! When "you are" is a feeling, subsequently any other experience is a feeling, too. Where is the question of happiness or unhappiness? Everything is a feeling only.

When you move around the world, checking out the advice from different people, various techniques, methods which you study, and then you come back to a certain conclusion, what happens to you, really? You remain the same, and you never see that this journey was not necessary at all. No advice is ever necessary from anywhere. There is no change in me whatsoever. You are only moving in ignorance all over the world, if you are closing your eyes and say "I can't see, I can't grasp."

So long as you are identified with the body, your surrender has no meaning. What is meant by progress? There is no question of progress, in the spiritual sense. To become more and more convinced about the guru's words, to get more understanding about your true nature is the only thing that matters. Other than that, there is no spiritual progress or spiritual path, because you are That. Only you must be absolutely clear about it.

The visions you get while doing meditation—what about them? Don't give much importance to them. Because the first miracle you have is that when you know that you are, you see the world also. It means that in your consciousness the whole world is present. Surely, that in itself is a miracle: to see the world with your consciousness. What greater miracle do you want?

INTERPRETER: They have been going to somebody for eight years; in spite of that they are not able to understand his language. And Maharaj is asking what have you done in the last eight years? Your achievement is that there is some God and you are a human being. That is your conviction; that is your only gain. So what have you understood?

V: Unless you meet the right sage, you cannot progress in spirituality, you cannot do anything.

M: There is no progress. You have to dissolve "progress."

You get conviction about yourself only when you go to a man of conviction. But who knows him? He has no doubts about himself. But they find it very difficult to understand him.

V: Have they read Maharaj's book at all?

I: Yes, but they have some doubts. Whether they are satisfied is not certain. Because only when you listen to him for a number of days can you understand. And in this way, you can understand more if you attend both morning and evening talks—that is the best. All your doubts will cease; don't allow any doubts to remain.

V: Many of the people who have come here have become *jnanis*. Maharaj has said that one should stay with the beingness-consciousness. Is that enough to automatically realize oneself or should one transcend the consciousness?

M: I am giving you an example. Suppose I am sitting here and you come. I come to know you are; then witnessing happens automatically. Has anything been done to make it happen this way? No, it is just like that. It is simple, you should understand. At some other time I have explained that it happens in the same way that a raw mango becomes a ripe mango.

V: Some gurus have taught or insisted upon the necessity for actually being in the physical presence of a realized spiritual master. Maharaj did not seem to say that. Yet, when reading the English translation of his recorded teaching, we feel we very much want to be in his company and there certainly is something very enlightening about his presence. Does he feel that that is important or essential?

M: It is very advantageous to get rid of all your doubts. That is why the question-and-answer session is required. So I want you all the time to ask questions. Otherwise, if you keep the doubts within, they will stay with you. This is the place to get rid of all concepts.

There is barely anyone expounding knowledge who is totally honest with himself. Normally, knowledge is given out with a view to getting something. What is that Self one has to abide in? The entire world is the expression of the Self. At the same time, the tiniest of the tiny, like an ant, like an atom, that also is the Self.

V: Sometimes it is called the mustard seed in the heart.

M: Beingness is like that sesame seed, very tiny. But its expression is the manifest world. The entire world owes its origin to this seed, the touch or pinprick of "I-am-ness." The seed contains the oily substance, which is the very source of love. Having provided love or oil to the entire manifest world, the remnant is that "I am." The pinprick or touch of "I-am-ness" is the quintessence of all essences.

Since you asked the question, many people having got the knowledge are not yet Self-realized. He who claims to have gained the knowledge and yet is still worried as to what will happen to him, cannot be considered to be a *jnani*. Have faith in the words of the guru, whatever he says. Here I do not repeat or imitate what other so-called sages are doing. I am not championing any religion, have no stance or pose for anything; nor even that I am a man or a woman. If you accept any pose or stance, you are obliged to take care of that by following certain disciplines related to that pose. Pay no attention to whatever other people have been saying. I abide in the Self only.

As to actions by other sages, I have nothing to say. No comment.

Whatever is happening spontaneously, let it happen.

Did anybody exist prior to me? When my beingness appeared, then only everything else is. Prior to my beingness, nothing was.

The layers of relationships pertaining to the bodily self are now being obliterated.

V: Does he mean the five sheaths as traditionally described in the scriptures?

M: Originally, I am untainted—uncovered by anything, without stigma—since nobody existed prior to me. Nor do I entertain any concepts about somebody existing before me. Everything is in the form of the manifest world, after the appearance of the knowledge "I am" with the body. Together with the body and the indwelling "I-am-ness," everything is. Prior to the appearance of this body and the knowledge "I am," what was there?

V: There was nothing.

M: The *paramatman* was there, the highest Self, the core of the Self. This identity is without any stigma. Even the sky cannot touch it. The space cannot touch it. It is subtler than space. It is just like sun rays or moonbeams: they do not get dirty in dirty waters. If such is their purity, what would be the purity of the Self, consciousness?

Understand this first moment, when we understood "we are"—the first moment of the body, when it understood "it is." Recognize that very first moment. Once you grasp this, then you are the highest of the gods, the point at which everything arises. At that very point, everything also sets: the source and the end are the same point. So once you understand this, you are released from that point. Nobody tries to understand this happening of the self, the happening of this "I-am-ness." Once it is understood, I, the Absolute, am not this "I-am-ness."

What did you understand?

V: That when the practice of dwelling in this "I-am-ness" reaches its fullness, there is no longer any containment by that sense of being a separate individual as indicated by the words "I-am-ness." That is how I understand it. But I may be wrong.

M: The only way we can express it is through words, there is no other way.

This "I-am-ness," the quintessence, the *sattva, parashakti*, is not "I." That "I-am-ness," the feeling of "I am," is the quintessence of everything. But I, the Absolute, am not that. That "I-am-ness" is the highest knowledge. And this is surrendered here by the abidance in the action.

I: A duplicate of him, who talks like this, you will not find anywhere else.

M: [*Addressing one American visitor*] Would you be inspired to put this into writing, these teachings?

V: Yes, I would.

M: Every creature in the Universe prays to that principle which he considers his God or whatever, but all this can only happen from the time the life force has awakened until the time that the life force is no longer working.

In the practice of meditation, this life force gets purified, and then the light of the *atman* shines forth. However, the working principle is still the life force. When this purified life force and the light of the Self merge into each other, then the concept, imagination, or mind, everything, is held in abeyance.

When anyone tells you to do some *sadhana*, with what can you do *sadhana* of any kind? It can only be this life force. The only instrument one has to do *sadhana* with is the life force. This life force, instead of viewing it merely as an instrument, has to be treated—mentally accepted—as the highest principle in the world: that is, God, *paramatman*, Ishwara, or whatever you want to call it. So that when this life force is pleased, it gets purified and merges with the light of the *atman*.

What is creation? Whatever has been created, is it the creation of God or is it the creation of this life force? By practicing meditation, diligently and continuously, this life force gets purified to such an extent that it attains divinity. Do understand that this life force is God, and God is the life force, and be one with it.

Now when this life force and the highest principle become one in your meditation, then whatever is reached by this merger, signifies the *moksha* or awakening, liberation, call it whatever you like. So what is *moksha*? Subjection to the *gunas* and all the other *upadhis* (the conditioning, obstruction) connected with the individual, all that disappears. That is liberation. This life force is the acting principle; and that which gives sentience to the person is the consciousness.

V: This is the traditional imagery of Shiva and *Shakti*[2].

---

2 Publisher's Note: Shiva is emblematic of God in the aspect of the Unmanifest, still, immutable Absolute. His consort Shakti (Parvati), is considered God in the aspect of the Divine Mother, representing the creation with its illusion of diversity.

M: Shiva is that speck of consciousness; and the working principle is the life force, the *shakti*.

People only go by the various names that have been thrown up and forget the basic principle. The principle is that within the body, consciousness and the *prana* or life force together are *atman*. I call it *antahkarana*, "psyche."

It is said that somebody is dead. So what has happened? The life force has gone and the principle behind the life force—that is, this consciousness—has also disappeared. That is all that has happened. I have been explaining the principle, analyzing it, for all these years. But from now on, I haven't either the energy or the inclination to explain all this again, so I can only say what is to be done, if anything. And the only thing is that nothing is to be done as is generally understood by the word "do," but merely to sit in contemplation and let the consciousness unfold itself, unfold the knowledge about itself.

You have done a certain amount of homework; that is why I am still explaining whatever needs further clarification. So far, what most people do is they explain only the surface position. You are to do *dhyana* or meditation, and in that meditation itself the consciousness will unfold whatever knowledge is to be revealed. But people generally don't go to the root of the matter and explain the principle, which is what I have been doing all these years. But now, I will also stop doing this for other reasons.

The Gita is a song, sung by Lord Krishna. What is it you want to ask about it?

V: I don't have a lot of questions about the Gita. It seems that it epitomizes some of the things that Maharaj has been saying to me very graciously over the past few days. I just wanted to hear his comments on that.

M: What meaning did you gather? What have you understood?

V: I feel that when *dhyana* is done properly in the way we are instructed, the first thing that becomes apparent is that this consciousness which is usually spread in a thousand different directions by our daily activities starts to get a greater sense of itself and then witnesses what arises. At the same time, the body's energy as a consequence becomes intensified too, and it seems to be polarized in a vertical dimension. I can't explain it any better than that. The other thing that happens seems to be part of the purification and what he was talking about was that we often...

M: I am talking about the meaning of the words, first as you have understood them, not what is happening. Happening would be an experience.

V: Well, that is what I have said; that is what I understand by the meaning. I also feel that many of the *Upanishads* and the Gita talk about the heart as the seat of the soul or where the soul enters this body; and beingness as something that is prior to this whole vertical dimension in which the life force moves. And even the life force gets eventually resolved in the center. It is like Maharaj's description of consciousness as a tiny seed and in that seed not only our body-being, but the world which we perceive, even the whole universe, has its seat. When *dhyana* is directed, the tendency of consciousness is reversed into the center; then that knowledge becomes resolved, the life force becomes purified, and is once again re-absorbed in that center, and you are free of that tendency to play into the world all the time.

M: This consciousness and the life force, when they merge they tend to become steady in the *Brahmananda*. And then all thoughts cease, even the thought that you are sitting in meditation. And that is the start of the *samadhi*. That state will remain for a while and discontinue again, whatever the reason. And then normal behavior in the world will start. That is, the life force will start its normal work or activities.

Now I am asking: This disease that I am said to suffer from, to what has this illness come? It has come to this consciousness and the working principle—that is, the life force. These two are concerned with that illness. And I, being apart from it, am not concerned with the illness. But it is one's duty to keep that life force in reasonably good working order. That is why the medicine was taken in the same way that the food is normally taken, so as to keep this consciousness and the life force in proper working condition.

So medicine is much like food. But as far as I am concerned, I don't really care whether this life principle and the consciousness work or not, because I am totally apart from it, beyond it and tired of it. The life force and the consciousness are not really two; as a concept they are treated as such but they are really one. As soon as a form is created, the life force is infused in that form and sentience is automatically present. There is a physical form and the life force, and in the absence of the consciousness there would only be a technically alive body. But merely that life force within the body—what is the use of it? It is like gas coming out of one's innards. No, it has no meaning, no function, unless consciousness is also present. So it is this consciousness which gives this life force, which would otherwise be merely air, the potency to create a sentient being.

People write to me, thanking me for my guidance and they say they now understand that although physically they and me are separate, we are actually one. All that, however, is still superficial knowledge which has been obtained by the consciousness upon its realization that it is not the body. But it is only at that stage that the knowledge has remained—on the level of words. They have not really gone beyond.

V: So they have just replaced certain concepts by other concepts.

M: Yes, you see, so long as that concept "I am" is still there, they have not gone beyond or prior to it; they have not gone beyond the total manifestation. So now when people come here, I talk with them. From what level am I talking? I am talking from the level that you are consciousness and not the body-mind. In my state, whatever comes out is from the total manifestation, not from the point of view of the Absolute. Hang on to that consciousness, which is your only capital, and do *dhyana*, and let that unfold whatever knowledge has to be unfolded.

I: Previously, he says, he had an intense desire to impart knowledge. So when people came and he found someone who was really interested, he even suggested that they stay four days, five days or a week longer. So that those who had made plans to leave would change their minds and stay on. But, he says, that was some time ago. Now if someone says he is going to leave in the evening, he will say leave now.

He gives an example. At a traveller's bungalow, people will come and go. The bungalow itself is not concerned whether someone stays for an hour or ten days. Earlier there was that little bit of desire left, not for himself but for imparting knowledge. But now even that little bit of desire which previously did not enter total manifestation, has gone and has become the total manifestation. That weak link between the total manifestation and the persons who came here has now snapped.

Have you understood this? Now there is no mind left at all—the mind to create a link between him and anything else. That mind has totally disappeared.

M: People come here. When someone goes to someone, there is a purpose. This may be for acquiring something worldly, or, as in this case, to acquire spiritual knowledge. So whatever the purpose, as far as I am concerned, they come, acquire something, the knowledge. Then, the person will say, I have got my knowledge now, thank you very much, and leaves. If I ask him to stay, it means I have some purpose in asking him. The purpose may be good, bad, worldly or unworldly, but there is bound to be some purpose. But I have no purpose. So if he goes, he goes; if he stays, he stays. Now the lady says: But what about the other person...I am not concerned with the other person; I am talking of one end of it. Not the other.

There is this "Adhyatma Kendra," which is a foundation created for this person, for spreading knowledge given by me; but I have no interest in that Center. What the Center does, whether it exists or does not exist, does not concern me. So now they have accumulated some money; they are going to give it to my family to build a house. So whether they do so or not, and what the family does with it is of no interest to me. I don't need even a house to live in; what is more, I don't need God either. I have no need of any kind.

July 9/10, 1980

8.

TO A *JNANI,*
ALL IS ENTERTAINMENT

V ISITOR: What counts only is what we do with the instruction received. The other day Maharaj was talking about *Brahmananda* and how during *dhyana* people get absorbed in that. There is something very different about a true sage compared with a yogin who becomes more and more absorbed and otherworldly. Somehow, Maharaj has broken through all that, and his presence seems very ordinary and normal, alert to the environment. At the same time you know he is constantly in a state of bliss, awareness, which is beyond our comprehension, and yet with this paradox of complete release and ordinary appearance. This does not seem explained at all by increasingly subtle absorption, where there is either consciousness of the world or absorption of consciousness.

MAHARAJ: [*He has just received some medicine and a list of do's and don'ts from his doctor.*] I am not concerned in keeping this life force alive, because whatever disease has come, it has not come on me but on this beingness. So from now on these do's and don'ts will be only according to whatever that life force feels like doing. And I shall not accept either the do's or the don'ts from the doctor. So whatever the life force feels like doing, it will do; and whatever the beingness wants to do it will do.

INTERPRETER: This question of medicines is mentioned by a number of sages who suffered from the same disease, or rather whose bodies suffered from it.

V: The most famous ones in my galaxy all had cancer—Ramakrishna, Ramana Maharshi and Nisargadatta. Their devotees explained that the reason these sages got the disease was because of what they assumed in terms of karma—a very crude explanation. Does Maharaj place any credence in that at all? It seems a terrible burden to bear.

M: As far as I am concerned, I have no experience of any kind of birth. Only at a certain stage I was told that this (form) had been born and this is "me." That is what I have been told—hearsay.

The ignorant man will want to live as long as he can. He would like to postpone the moment of death as much as possible. But for a *jnani*, what benefit of any kind can he expect by existing in the world even one more minute? So the only thing that would be nice is for the (vital) breath to leave quietly and not make a fuss.

The *jnani* is that principle which dismisses the life force and the consciousness. The consciousness and the life force together may be given the highest name and status; that is *atman*, Ishwara, whatever; but the *jnani* is not even that. The *jnani* is apart from even that highest category.

Having understood what the consciousness is and the life force is, I have never gone to anyone and asked whether my view is correct or incorrect.

Once you have understood the whole point, there is no need for you to stay here any longer. As to myself, having understood this life force and the consciousness, I do not have any interest at all in either one.

People have been coming here and I have been talking. Why have I been talking? Because the life span has to be spent, it has to be used. So even that is merely entertainment. Something has to be done; this is entertainment—whiling away the time, the life span. The name is the giving of knowledge; but what is the game? A game of cards, entertainment. The name is spiritual knowledge; the game is cards.

[*Addressing a particular lady in the audience*] Now that you have understood, you don't have to come anymore. If I ask someone to come, it would be common sense that I want him to do so for some reason. That he may give me some money or write a book about me, or do something which may be for my benefit. Normally, only then would anyone ask somebody to come. But here there is nothing of this sort going on; there are neither worldly nor unworldly benefits involved. So no one needs to come.

V: Tell him we like his entertainment!

M: The name and the purpose is spiritual knowledge. But the game is playing cards. [*laughter*]

V: Tell him I am no good at cards!

M: Whatever you have heard, have you understood and will it stay with you? And if it will, honestly, there is no need for you to keep coming. We are not preventing you, but you need not come. However, you may come if you want to...
[*The lady in question is pointing to her watch*] The lady's spiritual seeking is of a high order; she has golden bonds of filial and family affection. Everything is entertainment.
 Are there any questions?

I: Everybody is totally against Maharaj's consuming tobacco. He had one doctor after another telling him so. He says everybody is dead against my consuming tobacco. They say, don't have coffee, don't have this, don't have that; so he says he may reduce it but he is certainly not going to stop it altogether. And for what? Only to be alive a little longer, is it not? He says, even Vishnu, Rama, Maheshwara had a limited life span. Why worry about this?

M: There is no necessity to come here for any blessing. No blessing can be given to you. No change can be made in you. No instruction whatsoever can be given to you. You were perfect even before you came here. And you will be returning absolutely perfect, without even a dent on you.

V: One has to learn through one's mistakes then?

M: Who said that you have made a mistake? When you understand that you are perfect, only then do you know that a mistake has been made. This you can know only when you understand your true position; then you will know that mistakes were made. So when are you going to correct the mistakes? Is there any time?

V: Actually not. There is only the realization of it.

M: Any questions?

I: He is so confident you see, because whatever question you are going to put, you are framing it through your conditioning. And he knows he is beyond all conditions and can therefore answer any question. So he is always ready to answer you, and you are always trying to prepare the question through the conditioning of your mind, through whatever you have learned, acquired, all those things. So put any question you like, because he can answer you very confidently.

He confers such a profound knowledge through the few words which he utters, and he does it all in an extremely fetching manner. Now he says, I am just whiling away the time. I want to pass the time; therefore, I talk. Otherwise, I don't want to talk at all. That is his greatness. To a *jnani*, giving out the profoundest knowledge is also only whiling away the time, since he knows the truth about everything.

It is all happening in a dream; he is answering you in the dream. You are coming here in a dream. What is to be answered correctly in a dream? And what do you understand correctly in the dream? The moment the dream leaves, everything goes away. You see, he is absolutely certain about the true situation, that is all.

V: Does this means then that everything is preconditioned?

M: Did I suggest that everything is preconditioned? Nothing is happening; so where is the condition?

V: Then things happen by themselves?

M: Yes, in the objective way, things are happening by themselves. In your dream, the things happen of themselves or you make them happen. In the same way things are also happening here.

Whatever is applicable in the dream is applicable here also. If you want to call it a sort of system, there is no system that way. Very simply put, the vital force is moving; it is its nature to move. And whatever words come, the meaning of that word is the mind. Unless and until you have the vital force, you cannot speak, you cannot do anything. The mind will work only if you have the vital force.

Now take a scientific view. No work is necessary in order to initiate the state of knowledge. But when you are in a state of knowledge, you can do any work. You must not keep yourself idle; so do go on working. Whether working for the poor, the community, or for progress, whatever it is that you do, be at that stage of knowledge, of real consciousness. But when you ask me whether work will help in one's realization, my answer is that nothing helps there. Realization is first, then the work starts; duality is lost.

V: He knows that, he has experienced it. I do not have that experience.

M: Expounding knowledge is an absolutely rare thing in India. People keep to themselves and then disappear.

I have no explanation for the talks that go on here, the knowledge that is being expounded. It just happens.

V: It is the greatest miracle.

M: But note how few people take advantage of it; you may have observed this from your own experience. You must have seen a number of Indians come here. What are they coming for? For their *physical* well-being. What is happening is that these poor people are actually...they were to be dead. They are as though they are dead, but they have survived because of the company involved.

V: Are they doing any *sadhana*?

M: That is very difficult to say. Most of them are barely surviving; they are not very active. They suffer from poor health and can't come every day. But they acknowledge they are alive because of this place.

V: One of the things that seems to me an important guiding principle in my work is the determination of whether it is worth trying to maintain life when there is still a possibility of consciousness and that person wants to use it appropriately. Otherwise, I just can't see any point in keeping the body alive. I don't see it honors life at all.

I: You must have heard about his own daughter who expired. She was on her deathbed. So Maharaj, as was his normal practice, was going out in the evening. And when he was about to leave home, Maharaj's wife was also leaving at that time. So she said, "Your daughter is almost dying, why must you leave right now?" He said, "Don't worry, I will be back in a second; she wants something to drink, I shall bring her that drink, some cold drink." But upon Maharaj's return he found the girl dead. Then Maharaj kept the glass containing the drink on the table and looked at that. She got up and drank it. He said, I brought it. You had told me. After she had finished, Maharaj asked, do you want to live? She said no. And she fell down again.

There is no doer at all; no one has an identity to do anything. In the field of consciousness, everything just happens.

V: That is why it is so important that these teachings should become more widely known in the United States, for example. They are going to be very hard to swallow because there is such a strong sense of doership there and such a great deal of personal pride in achievement. The whole of society is structured around praising people and categorizing them in terms of what they have apparently achieved.

M: Here in India it is said that one in a thousand is desirous of knowing himself, and one in a million actually knows. There is some saying of that kind.

People who want only knowledge...I actually love such people, more than my own relatives. People who value Self-knowledge, they are dearer to me than my own children.

V: And he looks after them pretty well. Encouraging them and seeing that they are doing their lessons; they will be all right.

M: [*Maharaj is addressing himself to a visitor in monastic garb*] I am telling you that if you receive knowledge from me, then this dress will be of no use to you. You will have a less common dress.

V: Does it mean that I will take off the robe?

M: No, that will be your decision. On your own you will do it. Without my telling you, once you know what is the truth.

V: Is there no point at all in a methodical approach, like meditation?

M: No use. To reach this knowledge, there is no practice at all. No specific practice.

V: And it arises all by itself? Then, one does not do anything about it?

M: You know the world, spontaneously, without any effort. Or have you put in an effort to know that the world is?

V: I don't know if I put in any effort, but it is a mental creation, a reaffirmation of my own image of the world.

M: Whether you have put in an effort to know that the world exists or you just know that the world is—that is the question. Knowledge of the Self is also like that.

V: People teach that certain conditions must be ripe for realization. But then that would mean there are no special requirements.

M: Knowledge cannot be ripe or raw, like a fruit. You know that you are, that you have your "I"-consciousness. At present you wrongly identify yourself as the body. Body is given a certain name; that is "you," you consider it to be like that. But I say that in this body, consciousness is present. Or the knowledge "I am," as I call it, is there. You should identify yourself as this knowledge. That is all.

V: How about one's livelihood? Does it happen by itself or does one have to put in an effort to earn one's livelihood?

M: It happens automatically, spontaneously. Just as you wake up, and go to sleep, similarly, this also happens.

V: I have my robes on now, and if I decide to take them off, that would be another decision. Then there would be another condition, and I would do something else instead, and then in effect it would be the same.

M: Further, this body is also a covering. And you have to understand that you are not that. You are not the covering.

V: So that means in a way that the body takes care of itself?

M: The body is nothing but food.

V: But somehow we need food to survive.

M: Whatever food you consume, that is converted into this body, ultimately. And this body in turn is the food for the consciousness. So you come with the food, you come with the body. The question is one of correctly identifying what you are.

V: Advice to identify or not to identify with anything?

M: Instead of taking yourself to be something, you should know what you are, really.

V: I am going to Europe to visit my parents there, and I am certain they hold a certain view of me. And maybe it helps me in my situation just to ignore that completely. And perhaps they don't particularly like that I am in robes, because it creates a certain reaction in Europe.

M: But I am not concerned about these things. Whatever dress you have, that does not matter, so far as I am concerned.

V: No, not the dress but the attitude. For example, if I would take off the dress, just to please my parents, that would be consenting to their views about myself.

M: But that does not matter. You asked about yourself, your identity. If you attend these talks and then with the knowledge and understanding acquired you go back to your country, your behavior may not be as good with your parents. Your parents will not like it. So I advise you not to sit here.

V: If I try to really care about my parents in the way that I care about myself, to know myself, then the only way to be of any use to my parents is to make it clear to them that it is important to know oneself.

M: It is not very clear exactly whether you like this robe or not. The question now is whether you like it or your parents like it. Do you like this robe, are you satisfied with it?

V: I trust that if they like it, I won't feel any urge or interest to change.

M: Now what about your parents, do they like this? If you go around in this robe, will they like it?

V: I can't say because I have not met my parents since wearing this robe.

M: You come here today and tomorrow, and from that day onward you won't come anymore. Tomorrow you can still come.

V: Why is it that I can't come here?

M: You purchased that book, the two volumes [*I Am That*]; now you read it.

V: [*A new visitor has arrived and is asking questions*] I have read the Bhagavad Gita, Upanishads, and did some research in *prana*. How is it possible to arrest the disturbing thoughts during meditation?

M: Arrest the disturbance in thought?

V: Yes, the disturbance in the mind, during meditation.

M: What is the disturbance?

V: It springs from distraction.

M: What do you mean by meditation? And what is the distraction?

V: When you are concentrating on a mantra or on respiration, and there are many other thoughts coming in and you cannot concentrate properly.

M: You do not know what meditation is. The mind is the flow force. The mind is continuously flowing; that means the words are continuously welling up. When you do not get involved with the thought process or the flow of words, or the flow of mind, you are not the mind. When you are in a position to observe the mind, you are other than the mind.

V: I find it very difficult to do that.

M: For meditation, you should sit with identification with the knowledge "I am" only and have confirmed to yourself that you are not the body. You must dwell only in that knowledge "I am"—not merely the words "I am." The design of body does not signify your identification. And also, the name which is given to you or to the body is not your correct identity. The name which is imposed on you, or the name which you have heard about you—you have accepted that name as yourself. Similarly, since you have seen your body, you think you are the body. So you have to give up both these identities. And the indwelling knowledge that you are, without words, that itself you are. In that identity, you must stabilize yourself. And then, whatever doubts you have, will be cleared by that very knowledge, and everything will be opened up in you.

The indwelling principle "you are" without words, let us call it *atman*, the self. You are that self, and you are not the body. With that conviction, you must meditate, that I am that self only. The self or the *atman* sheds the body, which event we normally call "death." But to the self there is no death.

I repeat: The *atman* discards the body. It is the body's death, but the self or the *atman* does not die. But if one says, I am the body, then surely he is going to have death.

Who understands with the help of intelligence, hold on to that "who," not the intelligence. Catch that. *Be* that.

V: My question is, is there a useful way for arriving at *moksha* and are there particular signs for distinguishing which paths are the best for us?

M: You just listen to all this, whatever is being said here; follow that, abide in that and *be* that. Don't ask me about other paths. The path I am expounding, you listen to that, and abide in it.

V: How are we supposed to come to know this?

M: Can you not listen to the talk, can you hear it? So as you hear it, you *be* that.

As I said earlier, time is moving fast. Can you stop all your questions? You started very well; you asked very relevant questions.

V: I am interested especially in practice, how to start it.

M: Forget all about physical disciplines in this connection. I am telling you that the indwelling principle "I am," the knowledge that you are, you have to *be* that. Just be that. With that knowledge "I am," hold on to the knowledge "I am."

V: It is difficult to abandon attachment to action; even in this way it is not easy always to remember "I am," the truth of the *atman*.

M: You know you are sitting here; you know you are, do you require any special effort to hold on to that "you are"? You know you are; abide only in that. The "I am" principle without words, that itself is the God of all Ishwaras.

V: Is devotion not useful as an initial step?

M: First step or second step, I have the first and final step at the same time! The knowledge "I am," without words, itself is the Ishwara. He, Ishwara, does not want another (*Maya*) agent or intermediary. Direct.

V: The problem we are falling into is weakness of mind sometimes. This dims the awareness.

M: Who falls a prey to the weakness of the mind? You are talking from the body identification point of view. The real "you" is not the body. It cannot be cut to pieces by any weapon.

V: It is always the false identification.

M: If you identify yourself as the body, such an identity must be let go of, sacrificed. Your real identity has no body and no thought. And that self, the spontaneous knowledge "I am," you are. Since the self is not the body, the self is neither male nor female.

Thus, to understand correctly, you must be bodiless. You must be bereft of the body sense. It is no use trying to understand from the identity of body. You must fulfill this vow, that you are not the body but solely that indwelling principle "I am."

V: So in staying with that principle, there is no effort involved?

M: What do you mean by "effort"? And what would you like to have, to achieve?

V: I am still trying to be "I am."

M: You know that only, where is the question of any more effort? Effortlessly, you are that. Only you must stand for it with conviction.

V: Effort then is only concerned with the sense of body consciousness? Because one is still clinging to a body. It is kind of a trap. Why can't one really be in the state of "I am"? Because there is still some clinging and one wants to be free from that clinging.

M: You need not try to get yourself detached from the bodily sense. Once you abide in this, that you are the indwelling principle only and you are not the body—that is enough. When you have developed this firm conviction, where is the question of trying to get detached from the body identity? [*One of Maharaj's closest devotees, and also a relative of his, died a month back. So he gave the following example.*] That Mr. H. is no more. Now I know he is not. Similarly, you must have the conviction "I am not the body." Such type of conviction you must have, that I am not the body-mind, but only that knowledge "I am." If it clicks, it will click instantly. You see, I am not attached to any of you. Why I feel like that? Because I don't feel anything about my own self, and neither am I interested in this consciousness. Suppose that it quits. I am not the least concerned, because I am not that consciousness—a step beyond what I am telling you to follow. First of all, we are to abide in consciousness; that is the first step. Then I am not that consciousness either. And, this way of understanding should be shared in toto by everybody else. Even to say "understanding," is not the correct word—to abide in the truth. The way I do, the same applies to everyone else.

There is a couplet that states the real sage instantly transforms any devotee into himself, his true Self. The *jnani*—and he is at that highest stage—is stabilized in the destination, in the terminus. He is already in his destination. And because he is firmly stabilized in the destination, there is no movement for him.

We normally talk about various paths; paths are indicative of movement. I do not accept paths. You are in the destination itself. That is my teaching.

V: Yet, at other times Maharaj has admitted that there is discipline involved. He said that in *I Am That*, for beginners.

M: This also must be clearly understood that you are not a male nor a female. If at all you are going to say you are a male or a female, that means you are trying to understand yourself as body. This happening is like an accident. Suppose there is an accident and one limb is gone. You know the limb is gone; that is a bodily expression. Similarly, to call yourself a male or a female, is a bodily expression; that is, with reference to body—identification with the body.

With firm conviction, you abide in this knowledge "I am" only: bereft of body-mind sense, only "I am." If you dwell therein, if you be that only, in due course it will get mature. And it will reveal to you all the knowledge. And you need not go to anybody else.

V: Since I have been with Maharaj, this week and a half past, and through this very statement that he has just made, it has become very clear to me that it is the *sadhana* that matters, not the gathering of concepts that mean nothing at all. They don't change anything, they don't serve your liberation in any way. They are just garbage. The only thing, I feel, you have to follow your profession; that is, what your body is destined to do. Meaning can happen there. Ever since *I Am That* came into my life, that is the only teacher I have ever gone to. Until I was blessed with this opportunity to be in Maharaj's company. And I don't intend to go anywhere else.

M: Whatever you have said, I agree with; but why is it like that? It is because the Self cannot have an image. You cannot say I am like this.

V: Beyond any verbal formulation.

M: It cannot be consumed by the senses or the mind.

V: Maharaj said previously that it is not a question of cleaning the mind, but only of abiding in the process that is "I am That." In the very moment, for example, that I feel a preoccupation with my work, my art, my son or with something, in that very moment that preoccupation or that joy or that sorrow is disturbing my consciousness, I am That. Even if I know I am That. This preoccupation is the sensation that I feel.

M: Your consciousness is getting disturbed in you. Don't drag on, tell it succinctly. But you as consciousness should not get disturbed, because it cannot be touched by any conclusion outside. Because that conclusion is not consciousness. Let us suppose you have got a big bank balance, and something happens elsewhere. Your balance is not suddenly in debt, is it? Similarly, your consciousness cannot be disturbed by any disturbances.

V: So this means that I have not this consciousness. I believe I have this consciousness, but I don't have this consciousness.

M: That "I" itself *is* the consciousness; it is not a question of I am that consciousness, "I" itself is the consciousness. Only you are not to say that word "I." Without any doubt whatsoever, you are; that "you are" itself is the consciousness.

V: I have a consciousness, but I must *be* the consciousness, probably.

M: This is a subtle point now. In the morning you wake up. You know you woke up. You know the waking state now. That "you" who knows the waking state should be prior to the waking state, should it not?

V: Yes.

M: Now the moment you woke up, or you observed the waking state, you clung to the world as "I am the body."

This whole subtle thing must be understood. The principle which distinguishes or recognizes the waking state, that is the godly state. We know I woke up, clinging to the body; that is, the bodily state, the individual state, which is a downfall into a grosser state, because a *jiva-atman* is grosser [than the *paramatman*]: clinging to the body-mind as I am, in the waking state.

For newcomers I am not going to repeat my lessons again and again. You must be alert and listen to the talks with perfect attention. And then practice them.

For my own sake[1], my mind inclinations have almost come to a stop. There is no mind collaboration for me. Now for the sake of the public, why should I provoke my mind to expound?

It is different when you understand what I am saying. And I keep repeating, not everyone will understand me. If and when you understand, you will have to come so close to me that you will realize that all this is a complete illusion— that whatever it is because of which you see things is itself an illusion. Then you will throw up your hands and give up everything, since you are convinced that it is all unreal.

What is happening now is that whatever is seen is considered as something concrete and existing, and man wants to enlarge on it. Whatever he has inherited, he considers that that is something solid and worth having, and he wants to increase whatever his acquisitions are, whereas the truth is that he himself is an object and whatever he thinks and acts on, is itself an illusion. Therefore, whatever he acquires is bound to be an illusion. So man's whole view of seeing things must change radically. And only then will he understand what the truth is.

This consciousness itself is the source of all mischief, because once you start having this consciousness then that is the seed of wanting everything—having more and more wants, the insidious seed of mischief in the consciousness itself. And that is to be understood.

About hearsay, people keep saying things about reincar-

---

1 which means, at Maharaj's level.

nation, any number of births. But even the *jnani*, is he aware of even a single birth, that there should be talk of more than one birth?

There will not be a single *jnani* who can record his first birth. The concept "I am" is the primordial *maya*. And that *maya*, that primordial concept "I am," requires support and therefore God and Ishwara have been born. Along with that the whole manifestation, the entire Universe, has come upon it. Otherwise, there is absolutely nothing. And out of many *jnanis*, there will only be a rare one who knows the real nature of this primary concept.

I: He says, he has absolutely no need, no want of any kind, left. He has not got the desire that you all should come here and listen to him ...It is nothing; he is the Absolute, and in that Absolute he wants nothing, he needs nothing. And you will have whatever you will have; it is only an entertainment for your concepts. Whenever you come here, there are various concepts within you that will entertain you. But more than that, perhaps you will not understand all that is being said.

To look at him, he is an ordinary man, an ordinary body, but there has been publicity all around the world that he is a great philosopher; therefore all of you come.

M: But what am I for myself? In fact, that state of the Absolute is mine today—where there is neither Being nor non-Being. I have absolutely nothing to do with what this body is today. Whatever it has to give you is of no interest to me. So far as I am concerned, I am in that state where beingness and non-beingness do not matter at all.

You feel if I do this, I will get that. But when you understand the truth, you will realize that there is nothing; you are not. And so, whatever you get, what does it matter?

One has accused me of a very grave illness, but whatever is apprehended and whatever is seen is absolutely futile.

I have therefore nothing to do with this. I show you this truth, but you cannot catch it; nobody can.

V: Today, Maharaj has been stressing more the non-being of even himself, so I am asking while it is true that "I-am-ness" or beingness might be a time-bound thing and the result of some kind of illusion, isn't there something more real and lasting prior to emergence of this "I-am-ness"?

M: Whatever it was, that "I-am-ness" has become naught. Now whatever is left, that is the solid thing and is called *Parabrahman*: what was naught but still is.

Swartha (*swa* is self and *artha* is meaning) is a pun on the Marathi word, which means selfishness, and also "meaning of the self." So, how did the selfishness come in? That *swa artha* means I want something for myself. As soon as this consciousness comes on, all kinds of needs and wants start. Now, before that, what was the position? Before this consciousness came in, I had no needs, no wants. I was whole, without any needs. The needs and wanting started only when this consciousness came upon me. Once I knew the meaning of the Self, I realized there is no such thing as "I" as an entity. Therefore, who is to want anything? It is only while I thought I was an entity, because of this consciousness, that I wanted something; my needs were there. Thus, the meaning is twofold: the first is wanting something; and the second, subsequently, is not wanting anything because there is no entity to want anything.

I: What he is telling us is from his own intuitive experience. So what he says is the truth. But in the same breath he is telling us that what he states about himself applies to everyone of us. So if he says, as he often does, something has happened to "me," or "as far as I am concerned," he tries to keep us out but at the same time is telling us that whatever his intuitive experience is, it can be the intuitive experience of everyone of us. *Can* be. The potential.

V: That is why we are here and not with any philosophers.

M: Talking about philosophers, all these philosophers what are they doing? They are only acting philosophy. And all those concepts which are most dear to you, are images of yourself. Your image of yourself is that concept which is dearest to you. [*Referring to one of the visitors*] Now he puts on these Buddha robes. What is this but concept? There is nothing else there but concept. When you go to pictures, cinemas and dramas, what are you seeing? Are you seeing any original self anywhere? Acting, acting, acting. And it goes on endlessly. All playing their roles. Sometime, I am like this, the other time I am like that. And is any of it true? Nothing!

That which has appeared unknowingly has been taking on an infinite number of roles on itself and is moving about in the world like *Brahman*, Ishwara. But remember that this knowingness "I am" is not going to last.

I keep asking you to do meditation. Why? Because then that knowledge which is consciousness will unfold to us the mystery of the infant Lord Krishna. And what is this mystery? That infant Lord Krishna is this consciousness which is manifesting itself in the millions of forms. And it will come to us, or the knowledge will unfold to us, the fact that that which assumes all these forms in the world is itSelf really formless—spaceless and timeless. That because of which the consciousness is able to assume these various forms is itSelf timeless, spaceless, without identity, unconditioned, and original.

About the infant Lord Krishna—it will tell you how and why the infant body came into being; how the consciousness came into being, the illusory nature of this body and the consciousness; and that the original state is timeless, formless, and that what has come about is merely an illusion. Once you realize the truth that consciousness has come over you, you will need nothing any more.

Go back to your infant form, in order to realize that that which assumes the multitude of forms in manifestation is itSelf absolutely without any form. Those amongst us who have heard this and taken it to heart will get to the bottom of the whole mystery.

July 10/11/12, 1980

9.

EVENTUALLY, YOU HAVE TO GIVE UP THIS ASSOCIATION WITH THE CONSCIOUSNESS

MAHARAJ: People who think themselves to be in a position to air their knowledge forget one basic fact, namely that they go by mere appearances. Someone expounds knowledge and the one who receives it begins to ape the person from whom he has received the knowledge. Thus, whatever the teacher wears, he will wear; whatever mannerisms the teacher affects, he will imitate. And the transfer of so-called "knowledge" has been only that of concepts. This is essentially how tradition becomes established and traditional forms of worship come into being, all of which has nothing to do with the basic knowledge.

Whatever you have heard, whatever you have been told, will have no value as far as I am concerned. I want to know whether you accept the fact that the only knowledge that you really have is the knowledge that you are, this consciousness. Other than that, whatever knowledge you think you have, is mere hearsay, something acquired, based on that illusory consciousness. Is that so or is it not so?

VISITOR: To me it is so. The knowledge has radically stripped away the baggage with which I came here. I just don't have any interest in it anymore.

M: What is left is the basic concept that I am. That is the only concept that remains, and even that has to go. If you encourage it, it will build up all kinds of burdens. If you ignore it, it will go away.

V: I feel since I have been here with Maharaj that the one thing he has drawn me back to constantly is this absolute need to dwell on the sense "I am," and through that to transcend it. Anything else—I can think about it, say about it, do about it—will only distract me from the central command he has given me. And it is like this instruction I first received by reading his books, which is only being thoroughly confirmed and strengthened in his company; it is the key which is the verbal form of his grace to me.

M: In the end, one has to give up even the association with this consciousness itself. That is the ultimately aim.

V: That to me is when the paradox of his teaching comes in, as one is always making this assumption about oneself. And it is like the assumption has to undo the assumption which it is making about itself. There is that unfathomable element of grace that comes into this to make one stand outside what one is always doing in the sense of defining oneself as this "I am." It can't be expressed.

M: He who starts the search along a spiritual path expects to get something. But when he understands what I am saying, then the very need for something vanishes.

V: Expectation itself disappears.

M: One who will die with his ties of affection for the family, he will not be able to understand the gist of this matter, the secret of this knowledge. The ultimate conclusion one arrives at, if one understands the teaching correctly, is that there is nothing like an entity "I." Then where is the question of anyone wanting anything? So whether it is something worldly or unworldly, where is the question of anything at all to be sought? And by whom?

Consciousness has come upon one by itself, spontaneously. And that which has come spontaneously will go away in the same manner. So what is it that I can consider as my identity? That this consciousness has come upon you unwittingly, spontaneously, is it or is it not a fact?

V: It is absolutely true. I have nothing to do with the rising or falling of this consciousness.

Maharaj was talking about desire this morning and how for a man who is completely liberated, his home is the Absolute and desire comes to an end. What I am wondering is whether that is the case in an absolute sense? It seems to me that as long as this body-beingness is in existence, there will always be desires arising. Do they have a more lawful nature and do not bind for the man who is liberated? Or is it that desire truly comes to an end and the only urges that arise are purely for survival of his body-mind?

M: The *jnani* may do whatever he likes. Outwardly, it may appear that he has desires and is trying to fulfill them. But, ultimately, when he knows that he has no identity, he is the Absolute. Then, who is going to benefit from these desires, who is even concerned with them?

V: The force of desire is undone, that is clear.

M: After listening to this talk, what do you feel about yourself?

V: There are still desires arising in me that I am not free from. That is very clear, and also that this body-mind has its destiny. The main message to me of his teaching is that a life in the world and a life of service are perfectly compatible with the spiritual practice which he recommends. And the desires that still arise will lose their force, not because of any manipulation on my part but simply because I turn to this practice instead of the desires.

M: If you consider yourself to have a name and form, to have an identity, then the desires will have an effect on you. But when you know that you really do not have any design—no color, no name, no form—then on whom will these desires have an effect?

V: So often people when they begin a spiritual practice get very upset; it is commonly reported when you come in the graceful company of a spiritual master that these desires seem to get intensified rather than magically dissipated. And it is like Maharaj two or three days ago was talking about the life force being intensified and this purification taking place. What he was saying to me was that there is nothing you can do about those desires. This is what I have understood from his teaching. The only thing we can do is to turn to this practice with more sincerity, more intensity, and just leave the desires to themselves.

M: It is not necessary to wilfully ignore the desires. Just give attention to your "I"-consciousness—that is enough.

In the food essence the pulsation of the vital breath occurs. And the vital breath contains this beingness, that touch of "I-am-ness." And that touch of "I-am-ness" or this consciousness, with the help of the body and the vital breath, carries out all the activities in the world. If the consciousness were not there, nobody would feel the vital breath. In this organization, what is your identity, what are you?

V: I am that which observes it. From what I hear Maharaj saying, it is not that the vital breath in the liberated state comes to an end. Obviously, its play is still present in Maharaj.

M: You are observing what?

V: The play of the vital breath in the body.

M: At the same time, do you not also observe the consciousness? When the vital breath is there, the consciousness is also there. That consciousness or that "I-am-ness" is termed Ishwara, godly. When the vital breath is gone, that godly principle is also gone.

V: The presence of the animating force that this vital breath represents to us, the time I most observe its action is when I am doing what Maharaj tells me. In that sense of "I am" one feels all sorts of things happening in the body that are not normally noticed. I am not sure if that is what he is asking.

M: I am asking whether you are observing consciousness also? You say you are in a position to observe the vital breath and its actions through the body, the bodily activities.

V: I feel it can't be observed, the consciousness...

M: Can you observe consciousness also? How do you know that you are? The consciousness knows, the body does not know.

V: I think consciousness gets used in many different ways. To me consciousness is awareness itself. I know you use it (the word) in a different, more specific sense, but this is the way it is for me...No, I don't feel consciousness is like a thing you can observe; I think this type of definition of "I-am-ness" is a "gift" you want to know.

M: Do you observe consciousness, do you observe "I-am-ness"?

V: "I-am-ness," yes, sometimes.

M: For many hours you are witnessing the consciousness, that "I-am-ness." What this means is that you know that you are, that is all. Witnessing means just that. Since you know you are, you know all other things. First, the knowingness knows itself, knowing that "I am." And in the illumination by that "I-am-ness," or that consciousness, everything else is observed. I have had to repeat the same lesson again and again, and I do not want to run kindergarten classes of spirituality.

INTERPRETER: People go to visit and just have a look at sages; they are not interested in getting any knowledge, especially not this kind of profound spiritual knowledge. So Maharaj is saying since most of our people are like that, you can just tell them you have seen me and you better go now. He will not presently invite any newcomers. Previously, out of sheer exuberance, he used to invite people and say, come on, you receive this. Those days are gone.

He is in the state now in which there is no question of a god and a devotee, a *jnani* and people wanting to listen to him. That difference is already gone. So why should he bother about anything? From his standpoint, nothing is, everything is illusion, all of which he has already expounded in great detail.

V: Sometimes, it is just a matter of terms, not one of misunderstanding and sometimes I think when Maharaj's teaching is put in to English, more attention could be paid to using terms consistent with the way that most people understand them. Otherwise, the full force of those teachings will be lost.

I: These translations are in his own vocabulary of spirituality.

V: People have had to revert completely to using the Sanskrit words, and then spending pages trying to explain them. There just are not that many words in English to explain what Maharaj is expounding.

I: English English is different from American English.

V: That I know, because I was brought up with English English.

I: We, too, have a number of difficulties. Take the word *vijnana*, for example. *Vijnana* is used in physics and other sciences, but here that word is used as absolute knowledge. *Ajnana* is the lowest; that is, ignorance. *Jnana* is knowledge and *vijnana* is transcending knowledge, according to Maharaj.

M: You see, this "I-am-ness" is normally this five-elemental interaction and play. Out of the earth, with the help of water, sprouting of vegetation takes place. Out of vegetation, the essences are drawn and out of the essences, which are the food for all beings, come the grains for human beings. Now from the quintessence of this food, the "I-am-ness" is sustained. The food is stored in the form of a body. The food is continuously consumed by the vital breath. And in the process of consuming this food, the vital breath sustains that flame of "I-am-ness." To have "I-am-ness," the food body and vital breath are very necessary; in short, one may say it is a product of food body essence and vital breath. Then only this "I-am-ness" or consciousness is available.

Now the consciousness, when it gets involved with the body-mind, is the individual. It is conditioned by body and mind. Mind is concepts. Whatever it receives through the five senses, and is stored, that is the mind. And whatever the words that flow out, that is also mind. So when that consciousness is conditioned by the body and the mind, it is individualistic, a personality. And I always tell people, you depersonify yourself by not identifying with the body-mind. When you do that, you are that manifest principle; you are no more a personality, you are only consciousness.

When you are in that consciousness state, you are in a position to observe the mind flow, any thoughts occurring to you—you are apart from thought. You don't identify with that thought. Since you observe the body and its actions, you are not one with those; you are apart from that body. Thus, you are now in consciousness; that is the first stage. So when you are only consciousness, you are all manifest; this is to be realized. Then, provided you are, everything is, your world is, and your god is. You are the primary cause, the prerequisite for anything else to exist, whether it be your god or your world. You abide only in consciousness. In your attention, only consciousness should be there. That is the meditation.

Now the next step is—the question raised in the morning—are you in a position to observe consciousness? This is also the final step. When you are in a position to observe or witness consciousness—and, of course, the vital breath, body and its actions—then by virtue of that very observation, you are apart from the consciousness.

V: Maharaj has mentioned this on other days. Like the first step is getting established in this awareness of "I am," and being confirmed, strengthened and stabilized in that condition. Then one is in a position to witness what one always assumes oneself to be.

M: So when you are in a position to observe consciousness, you are out of consciousness. Then you are what we call "the awareness state," the *vijnana* or *jnana* state. Is it firmly stabilized in you, or are you still wavering, vacillating?

V: This central sense of "I-am-ness" has become much firmer since I have been here, without me having to go home, get my book out twice a day, read it, and then remember what I should be doing. I find I am being naturally drawn to it time and again during the day.

M: Is it not possible to remember that witnessing of the consciousness is to be done or is to happen? After reading the book *I Am That*, are you not able to conclude that witnessing of the consciousness is necessary?

Suppose you just got married; thereafter, you know you are different somehow, your status has changed: you witness your wife, you know you are a husband. Similarly, after reading the book, you know consciousness is there. Is it (the consciousness) not witnessing the consciousness? Reading is one thing, but actually applying it to yourself is another thing. Having understood my talks, are you able to fathom your own identity? Could your identity dawn upon yourself?

V: At moments, yes. Like the sun coming up at dawn, our overwhelming sense of it.

M: Can you understand the dawn? Before the sunrise, can you understand sunrise?

V: Intellectually, yes.

M: Not at all.

V: You can't witness it.

M: To the knowledge "I am," has it drawn a tangible, perceptible image? Is it very clear, this particular point? Then, how are you going to carry out your normal worldly activities? Since you know that you have no innate form, no design, how are you going to carry out, deliberately, your responsibilities?

V: I am not going to carry them out; they are just going to go on.

M: Have you been able to erase completely that symbol of birth that you represent?

V: Not completely, no.

M: Then, how can you state that you have got the knowledge?

V: I am not claiming for a minute that it is stable, it is...I am just saying that at times the sense of what Maharaj is talking about is overwhelmingly clear.

M: You apparently feel that you have understood the meaning of the words. But what is it that you have understood? For now, you might beam that ecstatic mood, but how long is it going to last, that blissful moment? It is like a flame, depending on the fuel.

V: Ecstasy is bound in time.

M: What is *not* time-bound? The experience that you *are* is time-bound. You know you are; it is a time-bound state. Consciousness means a time-bound state, and time appears spontaneously. This consciousness or "I-am-ness" is the time, which I call *kala*. *Kala* means time. With the appearance of consciousness, the ticking of time started. All this is the play of concepts. This primary concept "I am" appears spontaneously. It likes "I am"; it loves that "I am" state. Devouring ever more concepts, it gets totally enmeshed in them. And what is the source of all concepts? This primary feeling "I am." But never forget the fact that it is itself a concept, time-bound. And so it is all mental entertainment.

The world is an illusion, not eternal. Why is it unreal? Because none of the knowledge is going to remain permanently, as real knowledge. I had a number of identities: I was a child, I was a boy, I was a teenager, I was a middle-aged man, I was an old man. Like other identities that I thought would remain constant, they never remained so. Finally, I became very old. And then I had to be fed, you know, with a bottle. So which identity remained honest with me?

About the maturity you get with age—although on one side you get more mature, the other side gets chopped off, cut off. At one side I have aged so much, grown with age; but at the other side, I have cut off the remaining life. Whatever I had collected as my own, as knowledge, I have finally discarded. And nothing remains with me at the moment of death: everything is gone.

Right from childhood to old age, you have various associations—physical, mental and conceptual. These associations will not remain with you till the end; all are passing phases. Finally, the association of "I-am-ness," which you presumed to have with you constantly, is in the end also going to quit you, because that, too, is time-bound. Thus, when the body drops, that "I am" feeling which had been there from childhood, also leaves. So, that which is eternal and the truth, is something beyond the grasp of the five elements; it transcends all five-elemental states. Whatever is being witnessed is constantly changing. Only the changing state is being witnessed, but the witness is not changing. And when finally witnessing stops completely, there is the eternal state. This riddle will not be solved until you get the knowledge of your birth.

V: How is that possible?

M: Don't ask me; enquire within yourself. That knowledge about your birth you must definitely have.

V: True, but in this world, even if you are on the right path, or if you do good, you never get what you deserve.

M: What you think proper in the morning, becomes improper in the evening. The principle which knows that is not even contained in the book *I Am That*. It does not have that information. What is that principle?

V: No book can contain it, no words can describe it.

M: If you understand that it is beyond all words, then would you have that pride or ego that you are realized, if you are realized?

V: There will be no room for it.

I: To drive home that point, he does not just go along with the questioner, but takes an opposite line of argument, playing as it were, a special kind of devil's advocate.

V: That is his great service to us. If we still have an image that we want to present to him, we need to see that. He makes us feel it very strongly. If we truly heard and realized what he was saying, there would be no insecurity. There would be nothing in us that he could threaten. And yet there is. If that happiness in which there is no room for ego were truly ours, there would be no insecurity left in us—no fear, no anxiety. What I feel we have to pray for from his grace is to have the same impatience with ourselves as he sometimes shows us. And yet, great patience is there at the same time.

M: That will depend on your sense of urgency, your earnestness.

Without the vital breath, Ishwara or God has no soul; and without God, the vital breath has no existence. Whenever man limits his consciousness to body and mind, he is called *jiva*. Otherwise, he is absolutely independent of these two, which are acting and reacting. Consciousness, which expresses itself in various shapes and forms, is all one; whether it be an insect, a big boar, or a big man, there is no difference whatsoever.

Without the vital force, nobody can worship God. Actually, it is the vital breath, the life force, which is worshipping God. And without God, there is no existence of the vital breath. And without vital breath, there is no expression to God. Without this vital force, would there be even a reference to God?

When this life force seeks the consciousness as God itself, then dawns the light of the consciousness with which the life force works and achieves what it wants to achieve—that is, oneness with God. Even if you take the life force as God itself, the result will be the same, because the working principle is the life force. The consciousness is merely the witnessing process. When the life force carries on without any obstacles, then one is not even aware of this life force since it moves so freely and, therefore, you have a sense of well-being, you are happy. If there is an obstruction, you become aware of a disturbance in the working of the life force, and you have a feeling of unwellness and you are unhappy.

People are generally asked to do a certain *sadhana*, and as part of that go somewhere, visit this or that temple, or climb such and such a mountain. But what is really the working principle is the life force. And when you treat the life force as God itself, there cannot be consciousness without life force. So consciousness and life force are two components, inextricably woven together, of one principle. But consciousness is only the witnessing principle or the static aspect; the dynamic aspect or the working principle is the life force. Once you consider that life force as God itself, and that no other God exists, then you raise the life force to a status enabling it, together with consciousness, to give you an understanding of the working of the whole principle. But if you demote that life principle to mere self-identification with the body, then the life principle is not given the status which enables it to unfold itself. It depends entirely on you. If I identify this life principle with my body, then I make it work according to the body. But if I raise it to a godly status, and treat it as such, then that life principle will unfold itself and give me the necessary spiritual knowledge.

Earlier I had asked, what is mind? Mind is only the out-flow in words of this life principle, the *prana*. And how does the mind work? The mind is limited to the condition-ing to which it has been exposed; therefore, the mind can-not go beyond the specific molding it has undergone in the individual. Thus, the working of the mind differs from case to case. And about this *prana*, you have been asked to pray to such and such a God. So what does one really have in mind? Only the words, the designation, allotted to that God. But one forgets the principle and sticks merely to the words. But without the life force and consciousness, the words themselves would not come. Therefore, instead of identifying oneself with, and praying to, some word which has been given to denote the life principle, pray to that life principle itself.

Earlier I had quoted a couplet in Marathi, which says that that which is one's constant companion every moment of the day is the consciousness. Can anyone think of a sin-gle moment without this consciousness? So this is our friend which is with us for twenty-four hours a day. So pray to that constant companion of yours and not to some imagi-nary, conceptual God.

In my own case, with the life force not working so smoothly, what can anybody's medicine do? All that it can do is to try to make that life force work more smoothly. Now, going back to that old couplet, which says that this companion of mine—friend, philosopher and guide—who takes me by the hand every moment of my existence is this very life force. Other than God, what companion can it be, although the one who wrote it is probably thinking in terms of some conceptual God. Think for yourself: Who is this God who is your companion every moment of your existence? What can it be other than this life force and the consciousness?

People pray to God and when they think they do so, what are they praying to? Is it some idol, made of a material—maybe gold, maybe silver, maybe something else? But have you come across anyone praying to an idol representing the life force? This physical body, this apparatus, is generally regarded very highly. The doctors will say, anyone will say, that this physical body is a marvel. But can the body, however good, however pure, be as pure as the life force? If you make a friend of this life force—that is, if you identify yourself not with the body but with this life force—then will one need help from any other source; that is, from any source other than the life force? Is there anything more essential than this life force? If you have a choice by which you could have the life force or anything else, is there anything that you would give preference over the life force?

V: Well, the making of that choice itself would depend upon the presence of the life force anyway.

M: That is the point I am trying to make. That is why this constant companion is this life force, without which nothing can happen. When the life force comes into contact with the consciousness, this combination assumes the status of the highest God. That is, for one who has identified himself not with the body, but with this life force, can there be the need for anything else from any source? Has anyone been advising people along those lines? The life force plus consciousness—which has assumed any number of forms—is that meant for any one particular form or is it for the total manifestation, the totality of sentient beings? In other words, I don't have the life force, but the life force has this one form along with millions of others. Has anyone made any capital of any kind in order to pray to and please this life force? You don't need anything to pray to this life force. This principle has, deliberately or otherwise, generally been kept a secret from people who seek spiritual knowledge.

For all these forty odd years, I have been giving attention to individual persons. But now I have not got the time, the strength or the stamina to deal with particular individuals; I will only talk generally and people can make the best of whatever they hear. If someone does not like it, he can go.

V: My feeling is that if we hear him generally, all these niggardly little personal problems will take care of themselves anyhow.

M: Previously, I asked, if there were a choice: would a husband prefer his life force to his wife; would a wife prefer her life force to her husband? So far we have been using the expression "praying to the life force"; so I ask can anyone live without the vise—now I am deliberately using the word "vise"—of the companionship of the life force? I am employing the word in this way: the life force is the yoking, like of a bullock or a horse. In the absence of this joining with the life force, can anyone act at all in any way? If I decide to go somewhere, but my life force is not functioning too well, and therefore I am ill, then will I be able to go even with all the determination in the world? So, ultimately, even though I may think I am acting or doing something, it is the life force within which is driving me to, or preventing me from, doing something.

Millions (of rupees) have been spent in preparing an idol of gold, or whatever, the most precious metal; but if I don't have the life force, does it matter to me whether the idol is made of earth or gold? Or that there is even an idol at all? So long as the life force is there, whether in a fit working condition or not, whether well or unwell, the body is alive. But once the life force leaves, the person is dead; therefore everything depends on the life force.

Would you like to ask some questions? Who is eligible to ask questions? It is that one who has made deep friendship with this life force and this consciousness, who realizes the importance of the life force to the extent that he loves the life force as himself and not his identification with the body. Someone who has this love and has not identified himself with the body, he has conquered everything, and such a person only is eligible to ask questions. The union with this life force is in no way different from the love for the life force, the companionship with the life force; that is, this unity is love. Life force, love and consciousness are all one in essence. By all means, use your body to work in the world but understand what it is. The body is only an instrument to be used: you are not the body. You are the everlasting, timeless, spaceless principle which gives sentience to this body. This is the most secret but the simplest principle as far as spiritual knowledge is concerned.

I will give you a specific instance. In one who has understood the principle and is one with the life force, when this life force is ready to leave the body, what will be his reaction? Apparently, that will be the moment of highest ecstasy. Why is this? Because what is manifest is now going to be unmanifest.

V: What was said is to happen in the case of a *jnani* at the moment of death. However, it should really happen in the present moment when life is there, and not only at the moment of death.

M: That is extraordinarily difficult because a very slight identification with the body remains; it is extremely hard to get rid of that remnant of identification.

Words are used only as a means of communication at any particular moment. Time, space, whatever objects in the manifestation—are they not there because of the same principle? Manifestation is possible only if the life force is there; then only is it sensorially perceptible. If the life force is not there, as far as that particular individual is concerned, there is no manifestation, there is no earth, there is no love, there is nothing. The concepts we have carefully accumulated over a period of time will all be useless. It is this life force's conscious presence, without any form, which has been called God in various names. We have to repeat the fact to ourselves that I am not the body but the life force and consciousness; that is my nature. In order to know that, one does not have to practice anything; it is there, as an innate fact. Only after this consciousness has come upon me, I am aware of various kinds of needs and wishes and ambitions, happiness and unhappiness, pain and lack of pain; everything is only subsequent to the appearance of this consciousness. Before that, there was nothing.

The gentleman says he has come here to seek exactly what I am talking about. Of course, who will come to me for any other purpose? Self-identification—that is, identification with the body—is so powerful that I wonder how much of what I say will have any effect. And I do not blame you either. There is no limit to the extent of worldly knowledge that can be acquired. But all that is traditional knowledge which refers only to the world. To collect all that knowledge which has come down from the ages, one forgets who or what is really at the root of all this knowledge—that principle because of which knowledge of any kind can be acquired.

If one travels in the world, one must have all kinds of knowledge to make that travel pleasant and successful. But if one is not a traveller but merely a witness of the travel that takes place, why do I need knowledge of any kind? The physical construct which has been created as a protection for the life force, one accepts that as oneself. That is the whole difficulty. Knowledge in the world is helpful only to the traveller. If there is any unworldly knowledge, it must be of one's true nature. Coming to the theoretical knowledge that I am *Brahman* is possible only if one would stick to the much easier and simpler practice of making friendship with this life force itself. In saying I am the life force, progress would be very much faster.

Falls, accidents happen, bodies get crushed, there is loss of life and limb, but the life force is unaffected. Whoever has made this world and is concerned with its working is not worried about it, because there are innumerable forms which are ever created for the life force to work in. So if a few of them get crushed, the creator is not worried. [*laughter*]

V: Are *pranayama* and this making friendship with the life force the same thing?

M: *Pranayama* is a practice for achieving this goal. The son of a guru is not a proper son if he gives more importance to what somebody else says than what his own father says. In coming here, are you not belittling the status and importance of your own guru?

V: Is he angry about it?

I: Not angry but clarifying the situation. If a pupil considers God to be higher than his guru, then again he is not a proper pupil, not a proper seeker.

V: Who is conscious of this fear of death?

Second Visitor: The thoughts.

M: Which are? Who understands the process of thought?

V: The mind.

M: Who understands the mind? What is there prior to mind?

V: I don't know. There must be something, because it is holding the thoughts.

M: Yes, therefore I am asking you, what is it? That there is something, when do you have to say it? You know there is something, but you do not know what it is. You are able to say this or anything else only when you have the sense that you are, the consciousness that you exist. So stick to that—that consciousness which tells you that you are. Give up your identity with the body and concentrate your thoughts on the self, that consciousness which gives sentience to the body.

V: He means we are not body and mind?

M: Who has heard this, your saying that you are not the body? You have said that you are not the body, so who is it that has heard this and understood it?

V: I have heard it but not understood it.

M: You say, I have heard it, but who is this "I"? Who is it that has heard this?

V: Here, I am, sitting.

M: Now you are sitting here, you know that you are sitting here; so who or what principle is it that knows and understands you are sitting here? For a confirmed fact, there is no doubt about it. The answer is that the ego is this identification with your body, but I want to go prior to that.

V: How can I lose the identification with my body and mind?

M: What is the principle because of which you know that you exist and because of which you see the body and the world? What is it in the absence of which you would not be able to see your body and the world outside?

V: But I am still doing it here.

M: I will not insult your guru, because this is the basic question. And the answer to this question must come from your guru. Put this question to him.

V: It must come from the guru or must it come out from myself?

M: Whatever the guru will tell you is the same as that which comes out of your own self. That which you are seeking within you is the same as your guru.

V: It means the guru and myself is existence itself?

M: The difficulty with you is that you consider yourself as your body. And you consider the guru's body as guru.

V: That depends on my eyes, I can see only the outside.

M: Unless you recognize and understand that principle which enables you to see the world, how can you understand anything? It is the same basic question. Giving you the answer will mean insulting your guru, which I do not intend to do.

V: Did Maharaj get the answer from *his* guru?

M: Do I have to give you the answer to the question

whether my mother had a husband? How are you concerned? [*laughter*] You can't get knowledge by seeking answers to such questions.

What equipment you are having is that *prana*. *Upasana* means worship, worship of *prana*. For doing that, what equipment do you possess? It is *prana* itself. Along with *prana*, there is that knowledge "I am" or the consciousness. These two things are available to you to do anything. Nothing more than that.

V: What I understood was that we honor, we worship that life force by giving attention to the consciousness.

M: That is OK, that is the way. "I"-consciousness or that knowledge "I am" is "Great God," the Ishwara principle. And that *prana*, vital force, is Great Power or Great Energy, the kinetic principle without which there cannot be consciousness. Then that knowledge "I am" or the consciousness is the most needed, the most coveted thing. Everybody wants to sustain that; hence, all the efforts. That is the first thing. Along with that, you need so many other things. But the first requirement is that consciousness itself, the self-love. As long as you don't have the understanding of what you are, all the efforts and trouble are inevitable; they are automatically there. But once you get an inkling of what it is that you really are, there is no need for any effort, or for any trouble to arise.

In the earlier stages, there is self-love, but that love is formless. In the later stages, even that self-love goes. Then witnessing occurs of the self-love being absent. I am describing my state; it is something like a hollow stick, a hollow tube. No self-love being present, the love for existence has vanished; yet existence is there and activities are taking place. Like Brahma, Vishnu, or Ishwara, I have not taken any pose or stance, because there is no material to support it.

People come here and some do not understand; they argue, quarrel with me, fight me. To them, I say, OK, you are right, you need not attend anymore because you cannot understand me. The reason for that is your identification with the body, which you are unable to let go of. People will talk to me; they will do so only when something occurs to them: some concept occurs and the words start flowing. So whatever question someone poses depends upon what occurs to him at that moment. That person will identify himself with the body; he has formed the conviction that he is the body, and from that standpoint he is asking his question. But should I consider you to be a body while I am talking to you? How is that possible? So the questioner is full of color and design, whereas the one who replies has neither. How can they possibly agree? How can the questions and replies ever relate to each other?

July 12/13, 1980

10.

The Absolute Cannot be Remembered Because it Cannot be Forgotten

𝓜 **AHARAJ:** For those who have identification with the body, this knowledge has no meaning—it cannot act. Despite this fact, the visits these people make here will not be totally in vain; they will bear fruit at some future time. The effects of the visits will be like the aftermath of the rains: grass or plants will be seen coming out automatically, sprouting.

INTERPRETER: Many people come here to have Maharaj's last *darshan*, to see him at least once during their lifetime; they don't visit him for knowledge per se. He also said: "So long as I am visible, you can come and have a look."

VISITOR: It is what we cannot see that is more important. [*laughter*]

M: When somebody puts a question, he does not know to whom I am talking. He thinks that I am talking to myself. When a question is there, the reply is spontaneously available. The origin of the "I"-consciousness being known, the reply comes spontaneously. I am experiencing the world, but for that have I made any efforts? My true state—that is, the Absolute state—cannot be remembered, because it cannot be forgotten. Without remembering that, and without putting in any efforts, the experience of the world happens.

You have the memory of the knowledge of your birth; that is, somebody has sold you a bill of goods by informing you that you were born, and that memory stays very firm with you. Initially, you did not have this memory of birth, but your mother or your parent or somebody else rammed it down your throat. Subsequently, this concept was constantly reinforced with steady effort like driving a nail into the wall. As a result, that memory has become very strong with you; ultimately, this very concept is strangulating you.

In the absence of the beingness, when you did not know about your existence, both the world and the joy of the *Brahman* were worthless to you. They acquired value only when you came to know that you existed. In fact, until then nothing was of any value to you. This memory "I am" is neither true nor false; it is without these two attributes. That memory of beingness only appears to exist.

Without the knowledge of the body, that it exists and other bodies also exist, you will not feel better. In other words, you can entertain yourself only so long as you know you are identified with your body and consider other people also as bodies, not as knowledge.[1] Then only can you have entertainment in this world and pass time. Otherwise, how can you pass time?

V: What do you mean by seeing everything as knowledge?

M: When you no longer see the world as a collective of names and forms, as objects or bodies. Real understanding has no color and design. That is why, in so far as I am concerned, self-love does not exist. The love for existence does

---

1 Maharaj repeatedly states his view that "persons," in the absence of identification with the body, are consciousness or "knowledge" (of existence) only, or pure knowingness.

not exist. You may or may not believe this: the necessity to *be*, for existence, is non-existent.

V: I can accept that.

M: I am asking you, without body how to pass time? For a sage is that principle which is prior to body, timeless. How did he pass time? When the body was not there—that is, when the consciousness was not there—how many years passed by without knowledge of existence? It is a timeless state. When you witness, only then there is time. Time and consciousness appear together. Without consciousness there is no time, for consciousness *is* time. And there is no consciousness, prior to body.

V: But then what was there?

M: No, the question was how to pass time. Your question does not arise.

Sometimes you like to ask a question but do not know what to ask; you don't hit on the correct question, the only appropriate one.

The questions come up in jerks. Like a cat, you know, it touches with its mouth the udders of the mother.

V: We call it "bunting."[2]

M: Then what is the knowledge of religion? How do you understand this?

V: Time-suspension.

M: Your eternal, true state is your religion, *svarupa*. The word means "your own, true state." To remain in that is

---

2 Bunting is the activity of a lamb pushing its face into its mother's udders.

your *svadharma*, your own religion. All other things concern religions of others, not yours. For one who has no form, how can he behave in accordance with his religion? *Svadharma* means to abide in the beingness.

In this world we refer to some entity as God. That God, is he having any behavior? Has he any tradition—any rules and regulations?

V: I think all those rules and regulations are just a product of man's concept. The only validity I have ever seen in any religion is that for people who are obviously not interested in the highest teachings of truth, such as Maharaj's, these rules for public morality might confer some sort of order so that behavior is conducted in an orderly manner. Then, society becomes more cohesive than it would otherwise be with everybody selfishly going for what he wants—although that is what usually happens anyway. I suppose, ideally, it creates a platform of stability so that we may truly hear what Maharaj has to say to us. Other than that, I don't know...

M: For eternal peace you must dwell in yourself, know how this touch of "I am" has appeared. All other knowledge is of no use in this connection.

V: Certainly, organizing a religion is of no use.

M: When you listen to these talks for yourself, will you have any advantage?

V: It depends on what you mean by "self."

Well, the answer will have to be "no," because this self is to be undone, forgotten. To the true Self nothing can be added anyhow, so where could there be any benefits to it?

M: You feel like listening to the talks presented, although there is no advantage to it. Right?

V: That is putting it in absolute terms. I am listening because I have a lot to learn. We all want the state Maharaj enjoys. So in that sense, his talks are of great benefit.

M: I am trying to tell you: Give up all this trash, whatever you are studying in the name of religion, in the name of spirituality. Understand only one thing: That godly principle is there, that "I-am-ness" or consciousness—that is the godliest of principles. It is there only so long as the vital breath or life force is there. This vital breath has five aspects and is called *panchaprana*.[3] It is the motive force for all activities. When the five-aspected vital force is there, then only this quality of beingness is there, which is called *guna*. This beingness at present is your nature—you are that only. So worship that principle. That quality, the touch of "I-am-ness" or consciousness, is something like the sweetness of the sugar cane.

The sugar cane is there, the inside fibrous material is there, the juice is there, and the sweetness is the ultimate. Similarly in this case, the final thing is that quality or the touch of beingness—that is the Ishwara principle. You are that, abide in it and worship that only. Then only will you reach and abide in the eternal peace, and not by discussing any other precepts regarding spirituality.

A person got a baby; the baby was delivered to the mother. Unfortunately, the vital breath had left the body; the child was dead, and the body was disposed of. The question now is: What exactly did leave the body? The vital breath. But suppose the vital breath were there; then that touch of "I-am-ness" would have been present in the child; and that consciousness would have been there. The parents

---

3 *Prana* (Sanskrit for "breath"), the primal energy or vital breath, divides itself fivefold. "As a king employs officials to rule over different portions of his kingdom, so *prana* associates with himself four other *pranas*, each a portion of himself and each assigned a separate function." (*Prasna Upanishad*) The other four *pranas* are: *apana*, *samana*, *vyana*, and *udana*. The *pranas* are the essential energy component in such   physiological functions as breathing, digestion and assimilation of food, excretion, and procreation.

would have fondled that body, a live baby. But since the vital breath was gone, that life is gone, the beingness is no more there. And therefore it is just a dead body.

Where there is vital breath, the knowledge "I am" is present. There being no vital breath, the knowledge of "I-am-ness" is absent. Take full advantage of the naturally available capital with you—that is, your life force and the knowledge "I am"; they always go hand in hand. Right now, exploit it to the utmost. All worldly activities are going on only because of the knowledge "I am" together with that motive force which is the life force, the vital breath. And that is not something apart from you; you are that only. Investigate and study this exclusively.

Praneshwar means "the god of the vital breath." Now this breath or life force and the knowledge, that quality of beingness—both together are "myself." Fortunately, you have both these aspects together with you. You are that only. Therefore, abide in that, worship that only.

[*After some pause*] What concept is "bunting" at you now? [*laughter*]

[*Addressing a new visitor, who announces he has practiced Patanjali Yoga for twenty years*] In your study of yoga over the past twenty years, what identity have you found, what image have you formed about yourself? What is your true nature, have you come upon that? What do you earn your living by?

V: Interior decorator. Furniture design.

M: With all your study of yoga, Patanjali, and *sutra* for twenty years, have you achieved whatever you set out to achieve?

V: I am enjoying permanent happiness, twenty-four hours, non-stop, since twenty long years.

M: For what purpose have you come here?

V: Just to hear...[*inaudible*]...for telling you of my experience.

M: Those names that you mentioned, I have heard of them; I have not made a study of them, and they are only names to me.

You may have come having heard there is a *jnani* here. But I am telling you, I have no knowledge of any ancient texts, or anything. The only thing I know is this consciousness, this beingness, the knowledge that I am there. And I know how and why or in what circumstances it has come, and the value of that consciousness. That is all.

I started from the fact that I had no knowledge of the birth and how I got this body and the consciousness. I was surprised that this body and the consciousness should have come suddenly without my knowledge, without my permission. So whatever my thought and my knowledge, it started from there, inquiry started from that point. But Patanjali and *pranayama* and *kundalini*, all these are only names to me; I have never practiced anything of that sort.

V: I also feel it is not necessary. This Patanjali system I also tried, studying it from 1973 to 1976 without the help of any books or anything. I was trying to achieve mental concentration, since I felt most miserable; physically and mentally I was so disturbed that I wanted peace more than anything else. So that was my training. To achieve mental concentration, I went through a lot of trouble...went into seclusion, in one room, where I sat for about one and a half months.

M: How am I concerned with your whole history? It is nobody's business.

With all your study for twenty years, and having reached such a high standard, there was no need for you to come here.

V: Maybe I'll come once or twice, that is all—three times, maximum, that is enough.

M: Everybody is equal here. We are not concerned with the knowledge that you have acquired.

V: This is my existence.

INTERPRETER: Maharaj is speaking for himself. The other day, you may remember, he was talking about the resolution of his original inquiry, when he reached the conclusion that whatever knowledge he had acquired was all ignorance; then he got the final satisfaction and peace. A man with a keen intellect who comes here, within a very short time—say 10, 15 minutes—should be able to arrive at the conclusion that all knowledge is ignorance and that the personality is a fraud. But you are not accepting Maharaj's conclusion that all knowledge is ignorance. So Maharaj tells you to do a lot of meditation and find out: How did I get this first consciousness, this knowledge of existence? I did not ask for it, but suddenly, automatically, spontaneously, it has come about without my knowledge. How has it happened? Come to the solution of this mystery!

V: Originally it is there, that is why it has come.

M: When all the four Vedas ultimately came to the conclusion that it was beyond their power, what will *your* words achieve?

V: Nobody's words can achieve...No word can achieve this thing. When the word stops, what state is there?

M: If he thinks he is a *jnani*, he is wasting his time; only that person who thinks he has no knowledge should come here. But people like you who think they have knowledge, there is no use in your coming here; you are wasting your time.

V: No, I don't think I have knowledge.

M: No use your coming here, you are wasting your time!

V: I don't think anything like that. If somebody thinks it is a problem...I don't think...

I: Please...we come here to listen to his words, and we don't intend to make any comments that are irrelevant. Therefore, whatever he says and that is being translated...if you have a question on that...

M: What happens to the people who come here? They come because they consider themselves ignorant and want knowledge. So when they listen, they get knowledge and ultimately they give it up again as being unnecessary. But those who consider themselves to be a *jnani*, who consider that they have knowledge, they are wasting their time by coming here. For a person who is a *jnani* to come here...no *jnani* will come here. For coming here itself is an admission that he is *not* a *jnani*; therefore, it would be impossible for him to come here. Only someone who is in need of knowledge will come here.

What is the extent of my knowledge? Nobody will ask: Bombay, where have you come from and give me any details of it. Nor would Bombay ask anyone: Where have you come from and what are your antecedents? That is the extent of my knowledge. *Advaita* means unicity. In that, how can there be two: one asking about another?

I: Maharaj says his centre of seeing is no longer from the phenomenal; it lies in the Noumenon. But persons come here and to that extent we are phenomena. Therefore, in dealing with us he is forced to see and speak from the point of view of the phenomenon. Otherwise, as far as he is concerned, he is totally in the Noumenon. And so whatever happens in the phenomenal realm cannot and does not affect him.

People call to invite him and he appreciates that, but he says: "What is the use? I don't have an instrument with which to enjoy that hospitality or whatever is being offered. The instrument no longer functions. Anything considered eminently acceptable cannot be accepted because it has no effect on me since there is nothing with which I can enjoy it. But that is a position which I am unable to express, or is not to be expressed to others. All worldly wisdom and activities are directed toward acquiring worldly happiness. Whatever one sees, one gets interested in."

M: There is a couplet, which says that to anyone who is so interested in worldly activities and pleasures, how can unworldly wisdom even come near him? A person may read religious books and get interested in them, but for what purpose? Reading them gives him a sense of satisfaction, a feeling that he has done something worthwhile. He has done his duty as far as spiritual matters are concerned. That is all right so far as it goes. But what have you done to see your true nature? The five kinds of sensory perception, anything perceived by the senses, all that is only concerned with worldly pleasures. Sensory perception can give only pleasures of these five senses. There is no sixth kind of pleasure which sensory perception can give you.

One who has not realized the nature of the five elements and the five senses of perception will get himself involved and remain involved. But the one who has seen their nature and the way they work, will remain aloof and apart from them. I repeat: What is this state, before this knowledge "I am" came upon me? When the knowledge "I am" came, the one who is satisfied with that will reach the state where he considers himself God and *Brahman*. But he does not go beyond it or prior to it.

In the ultimate state lies the prior state; that is, the state before this knowledge "I am" ever dawned on me—the highest state, the best state, the original state. Consider the concept that the five elements and the three *gunas* are the lotus with these leaves, the little petals. When you remove its petals, then what remains? The Marathi word for lotus is *kamala*, and the last two syllables *"mala"* means impurity. So you remove the impurity and then what remains? Unless there is impurity, how can you see the purity? In pure purity, you will not see either purity or anything. Only through the impurity, can you perceive purity...then you see both impurity and purity. Seeing against the backdrop of purity...So here again is a further description of the one who has reached the delivered state.

When everything has been given up, and nothing creates attachment any longer, neither knowledge nor worldly pleasures, then one is in the state of deliverance. So that is as being the emperor of that original state. There is no attachment for that which is born, not even for that consciousness which is there. When all impurity of any kind, everything, has disappeared, then the original state is reached.

Consciousness cannot exist without the body, which is the result of procreation. So ultimately, is this consciousness itself not based upon impurity?

Earlier I had asked, if anyone comes here who considers himself to be a *jnani*, we will ask him, What is your age? He is bound to say so many years. Now that calculation, is it not based on the start of that impurity? Or, rather, from the day of the manifestation of that impurity? He who still carries the concept of his physical age cannot be a *jnani*.

Here is another example of non-attachment. A close relative and associate of mine died recently. Does that personality who is now considered dead have any use for me, do I have any use for him, does he have any use for himself? Whatever people may say about death, what has happened? Consider exactly what has happened and, therefore, don't be attached to him. This is an example of pure knowledge. That is, will the person who has gone, or whatever has gone, have any memory of myself? Then what is the point of my keeping memories of him, of that which has gone? There is nothing in the field of ignorance which can be pointed to as a comparison for the original state of fullness and wholeness, that which is. I repeat: Just imagine that state.

V: It is impossible to imagine. Any way in which we could imagine it, would belittle us.

M: It would still be a concept.

I: Maharaj is asking Mr. P. to show his proficiency with words, to explain what is inexplainable. [*laughter*]

M: This disease which the doctors say has visited me, is it not clear that that on which this disease has come is purely a phenomenal object; it is only on a phenomenal object that this can come. What is this particular disease going to do that would otherwise not happen? That which was given the designation and name of birth will come to an end. This is the only thing that could happen—with or without the disease. So what has this disease achieved by itself?

You might observe vastly different reactions from different individuals. One may be flabbergasted, downcast and horrified. Another may take it as a sign of the coming final ecstasy—that which will help to remove the burden of what is called "birth." Is it then not something to be very happy about? The actual pronouncement of the disease has achieved one thing: that knowledge which was very clearly understood had remained in the background and the phenomenal object was in the foreground. Now with this pronouncement, the phenomenal object has practically disappeared; this mere speck of consciousness is the only thing that remains, and is to go.

Who is to suffer the normal progress of this dreaded disease? Or what is to suffer? And what is its result? The result will be that that which was given the designation or name of "birth" may be wiped out. That is all that will happen. What is the normal process of fear? Any event that causes fear, if one succumbs to it, the fear envelops you. But if you do not accept it—the event as something to be feared, and you look it squarely in the face—then what happens is that the fear-causing event remains at a distance.

My teaching is very simple. There are two things to be understood. One is something I can see about myself, which is time-bound, proceeding from a particular point to a particular point. Beyond the latter point, whatever was perceptible will become imperceptible. The second is that my original state, which was imperceptible, remains. So these two states are merely to be understood; there is nothing else to be done.

Now I have a question: Through homeopathy, can you know the life force?

V: No, you cannot know the life force. The whole assumption by which one is able to get people well—and your experience proves it every day—is that a homeopathic remedy in and of itself cannot cure disease. We believe that what we do is just stimulate the life force to do a better job, or redirect what happens to it and by making a slight change, in the same way a catalyst does in a chemical reaction, you are able to heal where nothing else would work.

M: When you don't know that life force, how can you make any changes in it?

V: Well, we can observe it. With the machines we use, that is how we observe it. That is how we believe we have made a great advance on the traditional ways of prescribing homeopathic remedies, which are much more hit-and-miss and time-consuming in finding out what will work. But when Maharaj asks me, do I know the life force, I only feel it working in my own body in still very unrefined ways; that is all I can say. So it is not the sort of intimate, profound insight that he would have into its workings.

M: You cannot clearly know the quality of the consciousness or the type of consciousness.

V: Machines will never tell us that.

M: In Hindustani music there are various ragas; the experts know the differences between these ragas and can teach accordingly. Similarly, the changes in this consciousness, the types or quality of consciousness, can they be detected and explained?

V: No, I don't believe they can. Bodily changes, yes.

M: Changes in the body substance, that you can detect, but not in the consciousness.

V: And at a subtle energy level, relative to the body. But nothing more than that. I believe it can be known through experience, consciously, but it cannot be measured by machines. The only time we can see it, upsets on an emotional level hampering us, is when people don't respond. You know, you just develop an intuition about what is happening with a certain patient but you are not able to measure it directly. You just see their lack of response and know there is a tremendous stress input from those levels in their lives.

M: Whatever changes take place in the body substance, the consciousness is similarly affected; the emotions are also affected.

V: I believe that is so.

M: You cannot get lasting satisfaction from reading books. So you must try to know the seed of this knowingness, its very quality. Only then can you have this eternal peace or lasting satisfaction. But once you understand that, then what happens is of no further use, because there is no experiencer of all that anymore.

V: What is of no use?

M: That satisfaction, or that eternal peace, is of no use, because there is no experiencer of it. That is my state. Consciousness is the product of this body substance. So when you transcend it, then it is of no use to that ultimate principle. I call a *siddha* one who has attained the ultimate. In that ultimate state, the devotee and God, the *maya* (the primary illusion) and the *Brahman*, all these concepts cease to exist. And there is no beneficiary or experiencer of all that, because he is without the concept "I am." He does not know "I am," he does not know that he exists in that state. That knowingness is completely obliterated. The experiencing state begins only with the aid of knowingness. But knowingness is the product of this objective world, this objective matter, this food body. Through it that *sattva advaita*, atomic consciousness, is understood. Then it is seen to fall into the category of illusion. It is ultimately nonexistent, and thereafter twin categories such as god-devotee, *maya-brahman*, all these concepts—this entire world of duality—cease to exist. This love of beingness is there in all living creatures: the beingness is loved, that self itself is loved. But the love of beingness, where is the origin of that? The origin lies in that atomic consciousness. This known, only then can you transcend it.

People are talking about this devotee and relative of mine, one Mr. H., who recently passed away. H. represented the pulsation of something named H. So what happened to that pulsation, as he is no more there? That principle for the entity of which this pulsation manifested itself, has vanished. People have tried to explain it by saying that H. has gone to heaven, he will again be incarnated, and so on. Now, what is that thing that is responsible for the incarnation? There must be something, mustn't there, because of which the pulsations happen? The pulsation itself is the life force, but then we identify that as some individual.

This primary concept is the knowledge "I am." It is the mother of all other concepts. When this concept is there, then so many other concepts also appear. Now whatever religions there are, they are only full of concepts. Somebody likes a particular concept and passes it on to his disciples, and he gets a following. But with that, they cannot get eternal peace or satisfaction. In order to get that satisfaction, you must find the source of this primary concept "I am." And once you know that, you can transcend it. Then you do not have anything to tell the world, because the world wants only fragmentary modifications. They want activities. So this knowledge will remain only with yourself, and there will not be any customers for it.

Pulsation means movement; movement means air, the vital breath. Outside the body it is called air, within the body it is called the vital force. One who knows that state prior to the pulsation, he is the sage. When people come to me, I only tell them that you can meditate on Brahma, Krishna and all this, but instead of doing that, you should give attention to the knowledge "I am," and meditate on that by itself. Knowledge is to be got hold of by knowledge only. This will produce the seed which, through this process of meditation, slowly grows into a big tree and that itself will give you all the knowledge. It will not be necessary for you to ask anyone what is what.

These two entities are available to you, the vital force and the knowledge "I am," the consciousness. They appear without any effort; they are there. Now, in order to be one with Ishwara, to understand the non-duality, you must worship the vital force. Then that knowledge, which is in seed form, slowly grows. And the seeker becomes full of knowledge; in the process he transcends that, and the ultimate state is achieved.

V: What do you mean by "full of knowledge"?

M: It is the conviction about your true Self, intense and direct abidance in the Self.

July 13/14, 1980

11.

UNDERSTAND YOUR
OWN INCARNATION

Maharaj: At the moment you know that you exist; you are in the seed of the beingness, although ultimately even this very beingness is to be transcended. Everything is enfolded in that seed, just like a whole oak tree is contained in an acorn. Similarly, everything is contained in that consciousness: the whole world is there, and that body is also present.

"I am" itself is the world; it contains the entire world. That should be your conviction. Just as in a dream, when you feel that you are awake, but actually you are not and your world at that time is the dream world. Similarly, this knowingness (in the waking state) contains this so-called real world; that conviction must come. The truth is that there is no difference between (dream) consciousness and (waking) consciousness, although they appear to be greatly different; all consciousness is one.

Your consciousness itself gives rise to this world, which is a unified field, a unicity. But, it may be objected, there is such an infinite variety of shapes and colors in that world. How can Reality then be said to be "not-two," *advaita*? It is because all these differences exist only in your consciousness as appearances. The source is the same consciousness, but the manifestation exhibits so much variety!

The conviction that this world never existed can happen only to the *Parabrahman*. If this is indeed your conviction, then you are the *Parabrahman*. This thing aside, you should discover how this news "I am"—the knowledge of your existence—appeared and at what moment. Go to the source of it and find out. By looking up to others, to so-called "experts," and following them, or arguing with them, you will not get anywhere. Thus, only you yourself can find out the truth about yourself.

"You will come with me wherever I go." In saying that, I am referring to the vital force, *prana*. Make friends with *prana*, and the *prana* will help you to know God. The mind is only a witness; your real friend is the *prana*, because it does everything. Waking, sleeping, digesting food, all these activities are done by the vital force. *Atman* is only a witness; so give importance to this vital force and worship it, and you will be able to know God. In order to do any meditation, you should make friendship with the vital force; it is readily available without any effort.

Because of the *prana*, there is mind. And because of the mind, there are the *Vedas*. So ultimately, the source of this whole scripture is the vital force. That is why I give full homage to the vital force. Without it, what would be your value? Your body would collapse. Only when the vital force is present do you know the world, the world has value, and God has value. You can know about God and world only when the vital force is there. Who knows the greatness of this *prana*? That itself is God, Praneshwar.

As to the connection between mind and vital force, mind is the language of the vital force. When there is no vital force, there is also no mind. The words of *prana* signify mind. So how could there be mind without vital force? This vital force and the consciousness (that is, the knowledge "I am" or the beingness and the mind) appear simultaneously and always exist together.

Knowledge about the vital force is not generally avail-

able; it has not been recorded anywhere. So this information might be new to you.

Now that you have listened to me two or three times,
what is its result on you?

V: I know that whatever Maharaj has told us is the truth.
Now I also requested of him to show me a way. So he says,
sadhana is not the way, though it helps initially. But more
important, most essential, is determination. So that I am
practicing—it is a very difficult thing—and, with his blessing, one day I will succeed.

M: You will do a *sadhana* only until you receive the fruit of
it. Eventually, you will receive the result in the palm of your
hand. Until then you will do some practice. What, generally,
do you do spiritual practices for? What do you make effort
for? If you do any *sadhana*, you expect to get something out
of it. You say to yourself: this is what I want. So any *sadhana* implies a purpose; whatever kind of *sadhana* is done,
one does it with a certain aim in mind.

Now, who or what is the entity that is practicing? Who
is doing the *sadhana*? It has no form and no shape. So
where is it? It is within this form, this body—the indwelling
principle. For how long will it continue practicing? And
what is its aim? The aim is to abide in the Self only. Until
then it will continue the *sadhana*. Once it is established in
the Self, then the objective, the person who is practicing,
and the process of practicing, are all one only.

V: *Sadhaka* and *sadhana* become one only.

M: You see, when you make a *sankalpa*[1], what does it
indicate? Objective, the need, that is the whole purpose
of *sankalpa*.

---

1 *sankalpa*: resolve to accomplish something.

V: What do you mean by *sankalpa*?

M: *Sankalpa* means objective.

V: Intense desire and determination.

M: *Sankalpa* actually means "you express." What is the objective of the *sadhana*? I want *this*. Say, you want a medical degree—that is the *sankalpa*. Then *sadhana* is your practicing and attending college, doing the homework—all that is *sadhana*.

V: You made a *sankalpa* to meet him today. Then you came, walked, climbed the stairs—that is the *sadhana*.

M: *Sankalpa* (for example, that I want to meet him) has no form or shape; it is the objective and its expression. Now the one who makes this *sankalpa*, that one also has no form. For how long do you have to continue the practice? So long as you are identifying with form. Until then the practice will go on. Once you reach the objective—that is, you are not the body-mind, not the body form any longer—there is no practice anymore.

You have deep faith in the Bhagavad Gita. Is it not so? What is Bhagavad Gita? Gita is the song, sung by Lord Krishna. He sang the song, just as I am singing this talk to you now. This is his Gita. Now you are facing Bhagavad Gita. You read it, recite, remember it. But what is important: you must get to know that Krishna who sang that Gita. You must get his knowledge, what he is. Is he not an incarnation, Lord Krishna? He descended into this world: "incarnation." In short, from nothingness, the form was taken; that is what is meant by "descending into form." That is "avatar." Normally, for an ordinary soul, you would say that from nothingness the person has appeared: You would just call it a "birth." But in the case of these great personalities, great sages, you call it "avatar," incarnation.

It is good that you are studying the Gita. But what about that Bhagavan Krishna, who sang that Gita? What about him? Are you taking care of him by understanding him?

Now you are trying to understanding him through *bhakti*...it means you are creating certain concepts. That is not correct. From nothingness he is or he was. How did this happen? What was it that descended?

It is this incarnation that you must understand—the descent into avatar, into a form. Attendance of this beingness, avatar—what is this? That is to be studied and understood. Prior to incarnation, whatever that personality, he had no knowledge about himself. After descending into this incarnation, he started to deliver himself. Prior to that, there was no knowledge about himself.

V: Before avatar, was he not *Brahman, paramatman*?

M: Before descending into this avatar, this knowledge quality was not present; knowingness was not there. The "I am" was absent, not available. It is a non-knowing state. But afterwards, the state comprises all conceptual titles and names, and they are a person's shackles.

Suppose some convicted person is at large, and the government wants to apprehend him. So how will the government arrest him? Through the shackles of his name. If he did not have those shackles on him, would he have been caught? In the core of your self there is no imposition of any title or name. But, externally, on the surface, you accept it. Therefore, that internal core, which has no name, how can you arrest that?

What is the leash each man has? What are the shackles he wears? It is only the name.

Any person, any embodied person, with that knowledge "I am," carries on his activities in the world with the shackles of name only. If he had no name, it would not be possible to carry on with the activities. In that inner core, that knowingness or "I-am-ness," there are no shackles. Once it is understood that "I am" is purely "I am," formless—and not that shackled body form—then no liberation is called for. To be stabilized in that beingness, which has no name and form, that itself is liberation.

What I am driving at is the following. You are a devotee of Krishna and Bhagavad Gita, but do you have the knowledge of Lord Krishna? You know the historical facts about his birth, and so on; all that you know by heart. But you must know what this incarnation is. After this process of incarnation—that is, forming as the body—is over, then only this knowledge "I am" dawns in him. Then he knows he is, but in that prior process he does not.

All the beings, all the personalities are hauled into court and I am introducing this Lord Krishna as the chief accused, representing all. So I am talking about him. What is this incarnation? He represents all humanity.

V: If he was the Lord Krishna, what was he before he took avatar?

M: He (or it) was a state of peace, bereft of five-elemental play, without the five elements.

V: What we will be after death?

INTERPRETER: Whatever he is telling you relates to the Self, the *atman*. *Atman*, when he uses that word, is not that "I," the individualistic or personified "I." He sometimes says "we." Normally, he uses the term *apan*, which means "not conditioned by body-mind," something like "we."

V: I am "That"?

M: No, not That. "I," that core, without form and name. About that I talk. You asked me whether it applies to you.

What I say applies to the *atman*.

Understanding what that avatar is, the Lord Krishna avatar, means in essence abiding in that only. Then one is not the body. And what is the body? It is a mere aid for the sustenance or endurance of that "I-am" principle. To prepare the reception of this avatar (that is, the consciousness) this body principle, which is actually only an aid, an instrument or container, got ready first. Then, once it is understood—that is, when there is abidance in the consciousness only—this thing gets purified and also reaches the status of *Brahman*.

Now look at this example. You collected various types of vegetation. You started boiling this mixture, this essence. Finally, it got concentrated and solidified, assuming a form. Vegetable. Now the taste of that is something like the "I-am-ness" taste. This is all vegetable matter, the quintessence of all vegetation. Out of that, this body is formed, which is the food. And this food sustains that taste of "I-am-ness."

V: Who started mixing and who started boiling? Some power, some *shakti*...

M: Who made those flowers? What is that unknown power? That alone is the Lord Krishna principle.

So after incarnation, he got the form of Krishna. And that Krishna name, that particular personality started moving about and working in the world. But in the formation of this incarnation, what form was there? Or what was the agent? What was the aid?

V: That is just what I wanted to know.

M: Right now you enquire about your own form and the knowledge, that consciousness "you are," how did it come about? Was the form there prior to birth? Was it available?

No. Only because of Vasudeva and Devaki, Lord Krishna's parents, Krishna was there.

So the instruments for the formation of that avatar were Vasudeva and Devaki. Similarly, you had *your* parents as the aid or instruments.

And so long as both instruments, Vasudeva and Devaki, were not available, Lord Krishna was not available either.

Do you understand now that your parents are the instruments of your incarnation? Once you solve this primary riddle, all the riddles of the world are solved for you. Are you fully convinced about this?

Five ingredients with different tastes were mixed together. After mixing, a new product was created that had a taste all its own. Similarly, out of the five-elemental interactions or play, finally its culmination is reached as this body form and that "I-am-ness" taste. This is a very important step. This "I-am-ness" is the product of this objective world, of five-elemental play, from *vanaspati* to *vachaspati*. The former means vegetation, organic material. Out of that this body is there, and from the quintessence of this body comes the knowledge "I am." I call it *vachaspati*.

To repeat, *vanaspati* product is vegetable matter. But what is the quintessence of that? *Vachaspati*. The language or sound, what is the quintessence of that? *Brihaspati*, that most knowledgeable consciousness manifest. There only a human being reaches that highest state of *brihaspati*. Not other animals: they have no scope, there is no opportunity for them.

One who understands this process of incarnation will have gone through the entire thing, he will have studied all the instruments and everything. In this process he escapes or transcends that. And he is beyond that; he is free from everything.

The "I-taste" represents my father/mother. The quality of the quintessence of my parents, I am. The juices or secretions of the parents got mingled together, and the taste of that I am. Don't you understand how the incarnation of Lord Krishna also took place? I doubt whether this is clear to you.

V: It is clear.

M: The process of incarnation of Lord Krishna is exactly like this. So when the quintessence of the parents got consumed or exhausted, it is said in common parlance he [*the offspring*] is dead; and then the "I-am-ness" taste also vanished. Now can you get to know Lord Krishna?

V: I will try.

M: I dismiss this very idea that one should try, or make efforts. It is actually a very mischievous concept. It is enough to understand the core meaning of all this. That is all. Once you abide in the meaning of that, where is the question of *sadhana*?

V: If evolution is a fact, why were initially souls born in such a disadvantaged position that they had to keep improving, birth after birth?

M: You see, this is the counter question I normally put. If your next birth is decided because of your past actions, then what about your very first birth? I do not believe in reincarnation. However, I do not want to discuss that either, but if one insists and says the *shastra* says so, I will say yes, the *shastras*, the scriptures state it like that. I do not want to discuss further on that point, because it is adding to your concepts.

Right here and now, I want you to understand what is what.

That knowledge "I am" is not there after death; so where is any individuality left? So how can there be any question of further births? The fact is that nothing is born. There is no world. The world appears but it is not there. So you are talking about the next birth. But there is no birth at all; even now there is no birth. Understand Krishna! Krishna or any of the avatars is merely a happening, which has come and gone. You are not affected. So who is it that needs enlightenment? There is no entity that needs enlightenment. There is no such thing as enlightenment! After the body's death, there is *vijnana*, the absolute state. In spite of the body, I am in the *vijnana* state. Worlds come and go. I am the original being.

Enquire only about your own self. When your very birth is disproved, non-existent, where is the question of rebirth? Don't worry about the world, worry about your own self, about your own birth. These concepts—reincarnation, etc.—are meant for the ignorant. Once you settle this issue of the incarnation of Lord Krishna and yourself, everything is over.

For a number of years you have been studying; you have been active in this field of spirituality, but who is doing all this? That you are not taught. Whatever spirituality you may be practicing is full of concepts only. But actually who is doing all the studies? That you have not understood.

The reason that there is no realization in spite of all your trouble is that you are trying to identify with the body; you don't give up that identification. If you do not consider yourself as anything else, then at least consider yourself as the vital force. Identify yourself as the vital force and be like that. Other than the vital force, what is the most important thing in your body? Nothing; the vital force is the most important.

I will again give you a very good explanation of what is "mind." Whatever impressions you receive through the five senses, whatever you see, hear, taste, etc., all these impressions are in that vital force itself. They are ultimately gathered in the vital force—in the form of words: language is the mind. Whatever you have never heard, you will never speak. Whatever happens through the five sense organs, whatever is known, is "photographed" and accumulated in the vital force. And the language of the vital force is the mind.

Through the vital breath you perceive the world. And when you perceive the world, you perceive the five dimensions, or rather the five aspects, of whatever you observe through your five senses, and then it is recorded. That vital breath is therefore the most important motive force available to you. And when that vital force is available, it means you are also there. That "I-am-ness," consciousness, or beingness, and the vital force, both always exist together (like sugar and sweetness).

What is this vital force and that beingness? They form the quintessence of the five-elemental play. Being part of it, it has come to fruition as "I-am-ness." So don't try to make a fragment of it. That quintessential "I-am-ness" means everything. So when you embrace the body, that "I-am-the-body" idea, you make a fragment out of the totality. And this is the crucial mistake. Whatever experience you get, you study that experience, you understand it, but who is taking the photographs of all the experiences? Is it the vital breath? Where do you figure in all this?

For all the species, including human beings, this vital force itself is godly. And this vital force also contains that Ishwara or consciousness principle. Now you should find out: How are you going to focus your attention on that vital breath and meditate on the Self? That is for you to discover.

The vital breath gets conditioned or manacled by the bondage of name. It accepts the name as "I am." This is the mistake. That which is deconditioned from name and form is *paramatman*. That which is conditioned by the body, mind, name, and form is called *jiva*. The language of the vital breath is mind. And the mind is the motive force for all activities. Have you any questions on this aspect, this theme only? It is very difficult to ask questions at this point. If you are able to establish yourself in the vital breath as you are, you become manifest.[1] The vital breath, when it is conditioned by the body, you call it a personality. But, as a matter of fact, the vital breath is spread all over, it is manifest; it is universal.

If you are stabilized in the vital breath as "I am," that in itself will get you there. The vital breath is not confined to the body. All the elements are moved, operated by the vital breath. But because it is inside the body, you call it *prana*, vital breath. This vital breath itself is a vital energy. And that qualitative principle is the knowingness that is in the vital force.

It appears your studies of this subject are essentially based on whatever information you collect from others. That is a pity. The vital breath knows no death, and the indwelling principle, that qualitative principle "I-am-ness," it also cannot have death.

V: If I die without realizing I am this principle, what will happen?

M: You will die. In this connection, please don't use that word "I"—that exclusive, personified "I." You should talk without it. The moment you say "I," you are personified, you become individual.

V: This body...

M: What do you mean by "body"? Body is the food—the food for that touch of "I-am-ness," consciousness. Now take this chemical, whatever is fixed to that stick. [*holding a match*] That is the food for that spark. So long as this chemical ingredient is available, that food is available, and until

---

1 That is, the manifest totality, the state beyond the merely personal.

then the spark will last. It seems you never feel happy unless you get identified with the body. Get instead identified with the vital force, the vital breath, and then talk. Have you ever seen the vital breath lying dead as a corpse?

What is the vital, primary capital available to you now? It is the vital force only, and with that you perceive through the senses.

By worshipping that vital force, if the body drops (when, in common parlance, it is known as dead), actually do I die? Your Praneshvar, that divine vital breath, is it at any time apart from your body? Wherever you go, you are always accompanied. Who is your constant escort? It is that Praneshvar, that vital force. If there is no association with this vital force, can there be that "I-am-ness"?

V: In this life, if I do not realize myself and the body drops, what will happen to that vital breath?

M: You are accusing the vital breath. The body will drop, but what will happen to you, the vital breath?

V: Whether I realize or do not realize myself, there is a difference.

M: What does it matter? That is my responsibility, from my standpoint. For millions of years, eternally, I never knew I was. How did it matter? In the absolute state, that "I-am-ness" was not available. What did happen? It did not matter at all.

Because of the confluence of the vital breath and that touch of "I-am-ness," there are all these incidences of pleasure and pain. The cause of all that is this confluence—vital breath and "I-am-ness." Does the vital breath, *prana*, itself suffer pain or pleasure? No, but here that "I-am-ness" is lacking.

You talk on this thing; you only presume that you are a

jnani. What knowledge have you? Everybody takes pride and thinks "I am knowledgeable." You might attain any distinction, any elevated level, in this world, but this fear of death is not going to leave you.

This charge, that I am going to die, is it imposed on that "I-am-ness" or this vital force? The pity is until we reach that death, we always embrace the body as our identity, and therefore we have that fear of death. When the vital force operates through the body, that touch of "I-am-ness" is felt.

Now I am not going to talk anymore, unless you raise some questions.

V: Let me digest first what I have heard.

M: There is a simple fact. Where is the question of digesting my talk? You are the vital force. And the vital force is universal. That is all. When you thoroughly and truly understand anything without aberrations, where is the question of working toward further conviction?

V: What is coming between me and my enlightenment? When I have understood, I have faith in it.

M: Even "between" implies the idea that you are the body. That is the obstacle.

V: So I must practice to forget it.

M: Or visualize it (at once). Actually, it is not necessary for you to try to forget it. Once you say that you are the vital breath, where is the question of your trying to forget that you are the body?

Let me make it very clear to you. This body is the food; it contains blood and bones. On that, this vital breath is sustained; or, the vital breath consumes this food. And with the vital breath, this touch of "I-am-ness," the beingness, comes about.

V: Yes, in the morning Maharaj explained this very convincingly.

M: How has it been put to use? If it was driven home and has been understood very clearly, where is the scope for all these questions?

You are the *paramatman*, the *Brahman*. If that is too difficult, then at least try to be this vital breath, this universal air, only.

Is gold itself crooked? But when you make an ornament out of it—that is, you give gold a form and name—it becomes distorted or crooked. Just as by giving yourself a name, you became crooked. Gold as such is not stupid. Gold means the Self without name and form. But in gold, when it was transformed into an ornament and given a name, the distortion or stupidity started.

July 14/15 1980

EPILOGUE

Maharaj: The sum and substance of my teaching is this: Don't be dishonest to your vital breath; worship that only, abide in that only, accept it as yourself. And when you worship in this manner, it can lead you anywhere, to any heights—this is the quintessence of my talks.

Presently, you are to be identified with the vital breath. Then you will realize, like the sweetness in sugar cane, that this touch of "I-am-ness," which is dwelling in the vital breath, will open up. So understand these words, this advice. Assimilate it, and so long as the vital breath is flowing through you, abide in that. If the vital breath is there, you are there and so is Ishwara.

In such simplified fashion, nobody has expounded this profound knowledge.

15 July 1980

GLOSSARY

advaita non-duality, unicity

aham I

ajnana lit.: "not knowing," ignorance, spiritual unawareness; the opposite of *jnana*, knowledge

akash space; ether; one of the five elements

anatman non-self; all that is other than Self or *atman*

antahkarana the mind or "psyche" (literally: "inner instrument or organ")

apan(a) not conditioned by body-mind

ashram(a) stage of life; abode of sages and devotees

atman Self, the true spiritual Self, as opposed to the empirical self, the body-mind

Atma-jnana Self-knowledge; direct realization of the *atman*

Atma-jyoti light of the self

Atma-yoga the discipline or way of Self-knowledge; the practice that leads to knowledge of the *Atman*; path of Self-knowledge

avatar divine incarnation

bal-krishna lit. "child-Krishna," "boy-Krishna," a reference to the playful childhood of the avatar Krishna; in Maharaj's usage, "child-consciousness," the "I-am-ness" feeling before the formation of the mind

bija lit.: seed, "second creation"

bhajan devotional song; devotional singing; the practice of chanting and singing the divine Name, a typical feature of *bhakti* yoga, the way of devotion

bhakta a devotee; a person practicing the devotional path

bhakti yoga the discipline or way of devotion; the practice of loving devotion to God as a Supreme Being of love and grace

Brahma the god who superintends the re-creation of the world at the beginning of each cosmic cycle *brahmacharya* celibacy; more generally: psychological austerity

Brahma-jnana knowledge of *Brahman;* direct realization of the Absolute

Brahma-jnani knower of Brahman; one who has directly realized the Absolute

Brahman Supreme Being; the Ultimate Reality; the Absolute

Brahmananda the bliss (ananda) of Brahman

brih literally: "becoming great," "expanding"; "world" (in Maharaj's symbolic etymology of the word, *brahman* as *brih* + *aham*)

brihaspati in Hindu mythology, the "Lord of Holy Speech," the chief priest and guru of the gods, the deity of wisdom and eloquence; identified by Maharaj with a state of consciousness attainable only by human beings, "that most knowledgeable consciousness manifest."

buddhi intellectual faculty, power of discrimination; loosely, "mind"

buddhi jnana knowledge of or through the intellect; intellectual knowledge

chakra literally: "wheel"; one of the seven psychic-spiritual centers in the body

chetana consciousness

chetana-parabrahman the supreme or Absolute *Brahman* in its connection with consciousness; "the manifest *Brahman* or the consciousness *Brahman*

chitta mind, the faculty of thought

darshan the blessing derived from being in the presence of a holy person

dharma teaching

dhyana meditation

dvaita fundamental duality, the opposite of *advaita*

grihastha householder

grihastha asrama householder stage of life

gunas the basic attributes or energetic/material qualities that underlie and operate the world process; Maharaj also uses the term *guna* in the general sense of basic quality, and the sense of Being

Ishvara God; the inner ruler

janmarlana birth-marriage

jiva self, as conditioned by body-mind

jiva-atman individual self

jnana knowledge, more particularly spiritual knowledge

jnana marg path of knowledge or wisdom

jnana yoga the discipline or way of knowledge; the practice of contemplation on the impersonal Absolute as identical with one's real Self; *jnana marga*

jnani knower, sage, one who has realized the Self

kala time

kamala lotus

kundalini a psychic-spiritual power, also known as "serpent power," that in ordinary people is said to be dormant or "coiled up" at the base of the spine, but is, according to yogic texts, activated during the process of spiritual unfoldment, rising through the psychic centers known as *chakras* (which *see*).

madhyama literally "middle," the intermediate stage in the process of the manifestation of speech, between *pashyanti* and *vaikhari,* (which *see*)

mahatma great soul

mahayu(k) one who has attained union with the Self

Maheshwara a name for Lord Shiva

mala impurity

mana(s) mind

mana-shastri mind doctor; psychiatrist

marg path

maya the power of appearance, the force that projects the entire world of duality and causes us to lose consciousness of its true nature as *Brahman*; also refers to the world-appearance itself and, more particularly, the primordial illusion of identification with the body-mind

moksha liberation

moolasattva the most refined, most essential aspect of the mind's quality of illumination, the factor that makes Self-awareness possible (see *sattva*)

mumukshi one who aspires for *moksha* or liberation

muni silent one; sage; monk

murti consecrated image, icon

nama-rupa literally "name and form"; the world of duality, the entire manifest universe

neti-neti literally "not this, not that...,"; a saying from the

Upanishads that refers to the process of describing, or arriving at the Absolute by eliminating all conceivable attributes, based on the realization that all attributes are limitations that, in the final analysis, do not belong to the Absolute; known in the West as the *via negativa*

nirguna literally "without attributes"; the supreme aspect of *Brahman* that completely transcends the *gunas* or qualities that compose phenomenal existence (see *gunas*)

nirvana the state in which ego-consciousness is completely "extinguished" or transcended

nisarga natural, spontaneous

pancha-pranas the five kinds of *pranas or* vital breaths

para literally the "Supreme"; the source of thought and speech

Parabrahman the Supreme *Brahman*; the Absolute

Paramatman the Supreme Self

parashakti supreme force, power; the source of words or language

pashyanti the incipient state of the manifestation of thought and language, below *para*, the highest, but prior to *madhyama*, (which *see*)

prana vital breath, vital force

pranayama discipline of the breath; controlled breathing as a yogic practice; also, just watching the breath as a meditation technique

Praneshvar literally "Lord of the Vital Breath"; name of God in the aspect of presiding over vital energy and life itself

prani living creature; creature endowed with breath

prarabdha karmic destiny; the portion of one's karma that is being worked out in, and is determining the course of, one's present life

Rama a divine incarnation, the principal character of the Hindu epic, the *Ramayana*

rajas energy, passion, dynamic quality; one of the three *gunas*

rajasic having the characteristics of *rajas*, producing restlessness and passion

rajoguna the *guna* of activity and dynamism; *rajas*

rishi seer, holy man

sadhaka spiritual aspirant, practitioner

sadhana spiritual practice

saguna-bhakti devotion to God in the personal aspect, *saguna* referring to that aspect of *Brahman* that is "endowed with qualities" (see *nirguna*)

sakshivan the witness-consciousness; the Self in its role as transcendent witness of phenomenal existence

samadhi the yogic state of complete introversion or "absorption" in the Self, an advanced state of meditation in which one loses consciousness of the external world and experiences the absolute bliss and freedom of the Self

sankalpa intention, objective, the resolve to accomplish something

sannyasa renunciation, the fourth *ashrama* or stage of life in which the Hindu becomes a celibate monastic or wandering ascetic

sattva literally "beingness" essence; the name of the *guna* or quality of creativity, intelligence, and illumination that is operative in subtle form in all aspects of creation (see *gunas*); the quality of mind that allows us to be conscious and aware of the Self

shakti power, energy, force; the power, personified as the Goddess, that enables the Supreme Being to manifest as the universe

shaktiman the possessor of *shakti* or power; God as the possessor and wielder of the divine creative energy

Shiva for many Hindus, a name of the Supreme Being, source of the creation and dissolution of the universe

shraddha faith

siddha one who has attained the ultimate; accomplished, powerful one

siddhis psychic powers

svadharma one's own religion or natural duty

svarupa one's own true state or essential nature

tamas the *guna* or quality of inertia, resistance, stupidity, darkness, also the claiming of doership; one of the three *gunas*, (which *see*)

tamasic having he quality of *tamas*, producing dullness and lethargy

tamoguna the *guna* of dullness and inertia

turiya the fourth state beyond waking, dreaming and sleeping

turiyatita the state of *turiya* transcended

upadhi a superimposed adjunct or limiting attribute

upadro primary essence; victim

Upanishads the philosophical scriptures of Hinduism, articulating the doctrine of Brahman and Atman, regarded as a portion of revealed scriptures, the Vedas

upasana worship; meditation

vachaspati literally "Lord of Speech," a deity in Hindu mythology; identified here as a state of consciousness in which there is the knowledge "I Am"

vaikhari speech in its manifest, gross state as the spoken word, *para*, *pashyanti* and *madhyama* being its prior, subtler states, (which *see*)

vanaprastha the third of the four *ashramas* or stages of life, according to classical Hinduism, in which one retires from active life in the world; a hermit

vanaspati literally "Lord of the Plants," a deity in Hindu mythology; identified by Maharaj with the plant kingdom

vijnana spiritual knowledge

Vishnu, for many Hindus, the Supreme Being in the aspect of the preserver and sustainer of the universe

Vedas the most ancient of the Indian scriptures, four in number, said to be divinely inspired

yoga spiritual discipline, practice designed to purify one's mind and bring one closer to Self-realization

BIBLIOGRAPHY

Balsekar, Ramesh S. *Pointers from Nisargadatta*. Bombay: Chetana; Durham, N.C.: The Acorn Press, 1982.

Brent, Peter. *Godmen of India*. Harmondsworth, England: Penguin Books, 1972.

Nisargadatta, Maharaj. *I Am That*. 3rd ed. Translated from the Marathi by Maurice Frydman, and edited by Sudhakar S. Dikshit. Bombay: Chetana; Durham, N.C.: The Acorn Press, 1985.

_____. *Consciousness and the Absolute*. Edited by Jean Dunn. Durham, N.C.: The Acorn Press, 1994.

_____. *Prior to Consciousness*. Edited by Jean Dunn. Durham, N.C.: The Acorn Press, second edition, 1990.

_____. *Seeds of Consciousness*. Edited by Jean Dunn. Durham, N.C.: The Acorn Press, second edition, 1990.

_____. *The Nectar of Immortality*. Edited by Robert Powell. San Diego: Blue Dove Press, 2001

_____. *The Experience of Nothingness*. Edited by Robert Powell. San Diego: Blue Dove Press, 2001.

Powell, Robert. The Blissful Life. Durham, N.C.: The Acorn Press, 1984

_____. *The Wisdom of Sri Nisargadatta Maharaj*. San Diego: Blue Dove Press, 1995.

Sri Nisargadatta Maharaj Presentation Volume: 1980. Bombay: Sri Nisargadatta Adhyatma Kendra, 1981.

Offerings from

The Robert Powell
Advaita Library

From Blue Dove Press:

Beyond Religion
Meditations on Our True Nature
by Robert Powell, Ph.D.
Softcover   221 pp. $15.95   ISBN: 1-884997-31-7

In this collection of selected essays, reflections, and
public talks, Dr. Robert Powell— one of the foremost
contemporary writers of *Advaita* philosophy—addresses such
topics as Consciousness, Meditation, Existence, World
Peace, and the Arrival of the Third Millennium, and
addresses their relation to spiritual awakening and "human
consciousness transformation".

Excerpt from the book:
    What is the need for religion, for a so-called spiritual
orientation in life, at all? If living is a natural function, like
breathing, then why interfere? Why can we not continue in our
naturally more or less hedonistic way? This would be true if our
minds were still functioning in their natural ways, free of
complexity, flowing with life. This assumption, as we all know,
is no longer valid—if it ever was. Our minds are heavily
conditioned, fragmented and deep in contradiction. This conflict
in the mind leads inevitably to conflict in society, and thus to
chaos. So even if we opted for a simple hedonistic way of life,
sooner or later this would be compromised by the ways of the
mind.
    True religion or spirituality is nothing other than the
reversal of this whole process of chaos, conflict, to a state of
simplicity, naturalness, and therefore order...

Dialogues on Reality

An Exploration into the Nature of Our Ultimate
Identity
by Robert Powell, Ph.D.
Softcover   236 pp. $14   ISBN: 1-884997-16-3

"Dr. Powell is one of the best known Western writers on
Advaita *philosophy. He comments elegantly on the insights of*
Krishnamurti and Sri Nisargadatta Maharaj, and explains his
own insights on the nature of the unified state. You will find
great gems in his books."— **Deepak Chopra**
Author of *Ageless Body, Timeless Mind* and *Quantum*
Healing

Dr. Powell is widely recognized as one of the most
inspired writers on the subject of *Advaita*, the teaching of non-
duality. He takes us on a journey beyond the realm of the ego,
beyond the subject and object, good and bad, high and low, to
the ground on which the manifest universe rests. This is where
the mind and intellect cannot reach and which is beyond words.
Yet in this book, Dr. Powell does a masterful job clearly
indicating the path to where we have ever been.

Excerpt from the book:
"You see, the psychologist starts from the wrong basis.
His methodology is founded upon the assumption that there
really is a 'person,' an ego, that can be free, whereas what we
are trying to point out is that the ego itself, which comprises
both the conscious and the unconscious, is totally a composite
of falseness and the source of all trouble; it alone destroys
freedom and nothing else does...You see that you are not within
the world, you are not a small entity in a very large world but
the opposite is the case...The whole world of phenomena,
entities, creatures, is within my consciousness. And that
consciousness has no boundaries, no divisions; it is infinity
itself." — **Robert Powell**

Discovering the Realm Beyond Appearance
Pointers to the Inexpressible
by Robert Powell, Ph.D
Softcover   200 pp. $14.00   ISBN: 1-884997-17-1

"Drawing upon a rich and diverse stream of religious traditions from Hinduism to Zen Buddhism, Powell argues that the path to spiritual peace and happiness comes through a transformation to the advaitic mode of life....Powell ranges over such topics as death, reincarnation, religious beliefs, morality and spirituality. In fluid and accessible prose, Powell opens the doors to self-awareness through meditation and other advaitic teachings." — **Publishers Weekly**

"Dr. Powell is one of the best known Western writers on Advaita *philosophy.... All those seeking higher levels of awareness will find powerful tools in* Discovering the Realm Beyond Appearance.*"*— **Deepak Chopra**
Author of *The Seven Spiritual Laws of Success*

Excerpt from the book:
   "The meaning of your existence is primarily to realize your true nature, that you are not just an 'individual,' so that your life may stand in service of the world as a whole and make it a little less miserable. All else is mere entertainment, without ultimate meaning....
   "But once you have realized your true nature, when individuality has been seen for the illusion it is and so has been transcended once and for all, there is only the Totality. Now where could the Totality go? It is at once everything, completely fulfilled—it is fulfillment itself. Therefore, the question of meaning cannot apply for one, or more accurately, for That which has realized itself. We can only talk of 'meaning' when there is intentionality, direction, a movement from here to there, from incomplete to complete, applying to a fragment, the false image of an 'entity.' It could not possibly apply to that which by definition is Everything, Complete and Perfect in Itself."

The Nectar of Immortality
Sri Nisargadatta Maharaj's Discourses on the Eternal
Edited by Robert Powell, Ph.D.
Softcover   208 pp. $14.95   ISBN: 1-884997-13-9

"Nisargadatta Maharaj is my greatest teacher. His words guide my writing, speaking and all of my relationships. The singular pursuit of the awakened person is to find that part of himself or herself that cannot be destroyed by death. I know of no one who can aid you more on that journey than Nisargadatta Maharaj. His wisdom guided me throughout the writing of Your Sacred Self. *Let him be with you, as he is always with me, via this profound book,* The Nectar of Immortality.*"*
— **Dr. Wayne Dyer**, author of *Your Erroneous Zones* and *Your Sacred Self*

Sri Nisargadatta Maharaj (1897-1981), a revered master of the Tantric Nath lineage, is an inspiring example of an ordinary family man who attained complete realization of the Infinite. Living the absolute nonduality of Being in every moment, he taught that true freedom is a possibility open to every one of us. He drew disciples from all over the world to his humble loft in the tenements of Bombay.

Even on the written page, his words carry a special potency, subtly pushing us beyond the ego to our original, pristine and blissful Self, to the rediscovery of Oneness and authentic liberation in our Source.

"There are no conditions to fulfill. There is nothing to be done, nothing to be given up.... It is your idea that you have to do things that entangle you in the results of your efforts. The motive, the desire, the failure to achieve, the sense of frustration — all this holds you back. Simply look at whatever happens and know that you are beyond it."— **Sri Nisargadatta Maharaj**

Path Without Form
A Journey into the Realm Beyond Thought
by Robert Powell, Ph.D
Softcover   242 pp. $14.95   ISBN: 1-884997-21-X

*".... 'adventures in self-exploration'— but with a twist....
Readers versed in Hindu thought will most likely be intrigued by
the way Powell spins out its implications for authentic
living...."*— **Library Journal**

"This book can serve as a primer for spiritual seekers."
     — Georg Feuerstein
     Author of *Yoga: The Technology of Ecstasy*

"Dr. Powell is one of the best known Western writers on
Advaita *philosophy.... You will find great gems in his books."*
     — Deepak Chopra
     Author of *The Seven Spiritual Laws of Success*

"Recommended." — **American Library Journal**

Excerpt from the book:
       "The ultimate teaching is the seeing of the entire world
in not even a grain of sand, but a single point—and a point that
is dimensionless. That mystical 'point' then serves as the entry
into an entirely new dimension—the world of the truly
spiritual....However, for the individual embracing this ultimate
teaching, the vision of the non-duality of reality does not mean
that he has arrived. On the contrary, it is a mere beginning and
the understanding has to be tested in life's experience, so that
each moment is a new reality. This process of learning, from
moment to moment, is a never-ending movement. But without
that vision of the wholeness of things, nothing is of avail; we
cannot travel on the spiritual path...."
                                        —Robert Powell

The Experience of Nothingness
Sri Nisargadatta Maharaj's Talks on Realizing the Infinite
Edited by Robert Powell, Ph.D.
Softcover   183 pp. $14.95   ISBN: 1-884997-14-7

"Sri Nisargadatta Maharaj hardly needs an introduction any longer to lovers of the highest wisdom. Known as a maverick Hindu sage, Nisargadatta is now generally acknowledged to rank with the great masters of advaita *teachings, such as Sri Ramana Maharshi...,Sri Atmananda...,and the more recently known disciple of the Maharshi, Poonjaji..."*— **Robert Powell**

In this final volume of the Nisargadatta Maharaj trilogy published by Blue Dove Press, the ever-trenchant Nisargadatta uses Socratic dialogue, wry humor, and his incisive intellect to cut through the play of consciousness which constitutes illusion: this is his only goal. He can relentlessly pursue a logical argument to its very end clearly demonstrating that logic and spirituality do not necessarily stand in opposition to one another.

Nisargadatta uses every device in his command to great effect, turning his visitors' questions back on themselves, making them laugh at the very concept of "concepts" and ultimately revealing that the emperor "mind" indeed has no clothes.

Excerpt from the book:
"Everything that is there, it is fullness and it is nothingness. So long as I do not have that 'I-am-ness,'I no longer have the concept that I am an individual. Then my individuality has merged into this everythingness or nothingness and everything is all right."— **Sri Nisargadatta Maharaj**